# Marcie Davis & Melissa Bunnell

# Working Like DOGS

## The Service Dog Guidebook

### Alpine
**PUBLICATIONS**
Crawford, CO 81415

Cataloging in Publication Data

   Davis, Marcie   1965-
    Working like dogs : the service dog guidebook / Marcie Davis, Melissa Bunell
       p. cm.
    Includes bibliographical references and index.
    ISBN 978-1-57779-086-0 (pbk.)  --  ISBN 978-1-57779-087-1 (wire bound)
       1. Service dogs.  I. Bunnell, Melissa, 1968-   II. Title

   HV1569.6.D38 2007
   362.4'0483—dc22

                2006103489

Design and layout: Laura Newport
Cover Photo: Doug Reeves
Editing: Kathryn Stewart
Photographs: Doug Reeves, Franz Freibert, Kim Alaburda, Assistance Dogs of the West, Alicia Chatman, International Hearing Dogs, Inc., Kenny Hosack.

First printing

   4  5  6  7  8  9  0

Printed in the United States of America.

# CONTENTS

*Courtesy of Alicia Chatman.*

# FOREWORD

In the seventies I had the privilege of meeting and getting to know the very first trained service dog, a smallish black Labrador named Abdul. He belonged to Kerrill Knaus, a paraplegic. They were guests on my television program to show the many ways Abdul assisted his partner in things she couldn't do for herself – turning lights on and off, picking up dropped objects, pushing elevator buttons, fetching items from the fridge – the list goes on. All things that we take for granted.

At the same time I met Bonnie Bergin, who worked with Kerry in training Abdul. It was Bonnie's dream to build a national program for these dogs – similar to those for dogs who lead the blind. It was a tough uphill battle with much initial opposition, but today Dr. Bonnie Bergin's dream has become an international reality.

At last, this fine book helps us realize what the term "service dog" really means and appreciate the different worlds these animals have opened for their partners, physically, psychologically, emotionally, and socially.

Abdul and Kerry were together for sixteen years and I am proud to say Kerry's and my friendship continues. She has built her own organization, H.O.R.S.E.S. – Adaptive Riding Institute for the Physically Challenged. Abdul would be very proud to know all the good work he started.

Enjoy this good read and, thanks to Marcie and Melissa, the next time you see a wheelchair with a dog walking beside it you'll know you are witnessing a true partnership in action.

Betty White
Actress/Author

*Photo © Doug Reeves*

# PREFACE

Have you ever been at a shopping mall or some other public place and happened to witness a person with a disability accompanied by a service dog? And on seeing this wonderful sight, did you have the irresistible urge to approach that person to ask a million questions? "How did you get your dog? What does the dog do for you? How old is the dog and what age will the dog be able to work? Have you had the dog since it was a puppy? Did you get to name the dog?" Or did you just sit in awe and watch as this human/canine team performed tasks with such simplicity and grace that you knew they must be reading each others' minds? In this book we hope to answer all of your questions and many more.

I (Marcie) received my first service dog, Ramona, in 1993 and have been partnered with my second service dog, Morgan, since 2000. I am now anticipating Morgan's retirement and the arrival of my third service dog. As a service dog recipient, I wish this book had been available to aid in my decision about getting a service dog and to support the decisions I would have to make throughout the lives of my service dogs. Little did I know how much my life would change or how much I would come to depend upon and love the magnificent creature who was my helper. Dealing with the loss of Ramona was something I was totally unprepared for and I had no idea where to turn for support. I sought the help of a close friend and colleague, Melissa Bunnell, who specializes in crisis counseling. Because helping others deal with the grief and the loss of their assistance dog is just as important to me as helping them decide on a dog in the first place, we embarked on a journey to create Working Like Dogs, LLC, an organization dedicated to honoring and celebrating assistance dogs around the world. Since 2001, we have worked together to research, write, and develop resources to be of assistance to service dog recipients, puppy raisers, and trainers.

In writing this book we will provide you with a window into the magical relationship between a human and their service dog partner. The information on which this book is based was generated from personal experiences with my (Marcie's) service dogs. Service dogs are just one type of assistance dogs. Much of the information we provide can apply to other types of assistance dogs as well. Assistance dogs and service dogs are defined in Chapter 1; however, we use the terms "assistance dog" and "service dog" somewhat interchangeably after that, depending upon the context. You will see the term "service dog" more often because we based this book on my personal experiences and I have mobility limitations. Keep in mind that the Americans with Disabilities Act (ADA) treats all assistance dogs equally.

We hope this book will provide you with pertinent information whether you are trying to decide if a service dog is right for you; if you are already a proud recipient; or if you just want to learn more about service dogs. As well as providing you with valuable information on everything from how and where to apply for a dog to daily care and health concerns and eventually preparing for a successor, each chapter contains elements from my personal experiences. Stories of other assistance dog recipients are also included to help you gain insight into the realities of this amazing symbiotic relationship between human and canine.

We hope this book will assist you in your decisions, in your relationships with your canine companions, and in your life.

Marcie Davis and Melissa Bunnell
2007

This book is dedicated to
Ramona and Morgan,
two special service dogs that
changed our lives.

Thank you for
your selfless love
and devotion.

# ACKNOWLEDGEMENTS

## MARCIE DAVIS

To the three special gifts in my life – husband, Franz, and service dogs, Ramona and Morgan. Each of these individuals has touched my life in ways that can never be expressed and has enabled me to live a productive and meaningful life. This work was created because of their unwavering support.

I would also like to thank Canine Companions for Independence and Paws With A Cause for their commitment to training and placing amazing service dogs. You have touched the lives of so many.

To Melissa, thank you for being such a dear and gentle spirit and for sharing the love of this project with me.

## MELISSA BUNNELL

I would like to thank my parents, David and Patricia Bunnell, who always believed I could be whatever I wanted to be. Special thanks to my dear husband Peter Mitchell for his unwavering faith in me and in the potential of this book, and to my daughter, Leah, who is a daily inspiration to do good work. To Morgan, Ramona, and all service dogs whose tireless work and remarkable skill make this world a better and more accessible place, and to my co-author and friend, Marcie, a fearless and formidable advocate and activist and one heck of a writing partner.

Together, we would like to thank our publisher, Betty McKinney at Alpine Publications, for making our dream a reality; Jeff, Sherry, Donna, Kevin, and Shelley for sharing their personal assistance dog experiences; Doug Reeves, Kim Alaburda and Franz Freibert for capturing the spirit of the service dog partnership through their photographs; Paws With A Cause, Assistance Dogs of the West, International Hearing Dogs, Inc., and a special thank you to Franz Freibert for his diligence and commitment to helping us create this manuscript.

# CHAPTER ONE
## An Introduction to Assistance Dogs

Assistance dogs are dogs of many different breeds that have been individually selected and trained to aid individuals with disabilities. Assistance dogs are task-trained and may include: service dogs, guide dogs, hearing alert and seizure alert/seizure response dogs. Assistance dog tasks and commands vary from agency to agency and disability to disability. Most assistance dog tasks fall into three basic categories: basic obedience, service tasks, and public access. These specially trained dogs assist individuals with disabilities and accomplish tasks such as answering the phone or doorbell, retrieving items, alerting to physical problems, carrying items in a pack, assisting their owners while crossing streets, negotiating stairways and elevators, and a host of other daily tasks. I, Marcie, am a paraplegic which means I am paralyzed from the waist down. As a result, I use a power wheelchair for 100% of my mobility. Therefore, I need a service dog to assist me with physical mobility tasks such as picking up things that I drop or cannot reach, helping me get into bed and covering me up, opening and closing doors, getting the telephone, turning light switches on and off, and pushing elevator buttons. I was partnered with my first service dog, Ramona, in 1993, my second dog, Morgan, in 2000, and I am now anticipating Morgan's retirement and the arrival of my third service dog sometime in 2007.

## HISTORY OF ASSISTANCE DOGS

Since the 18th century, individuals with vision loss have utilized dogs to improve their mobility. The precipitating event in history that led to the establishment of the first recognized training program for guide dogs was World War I. The first formal school for dogs to assist people who are blind was reportedly founded in Pottsdam, Germany, to serve war veterans who were blind. Dorothy Harrison Eustis, a German Shepherd breeder living in Switzerland, heard about the school and visited it. On November 5, 1927, Ms. Eutis published an article in *The Saturday Evening Post* describing her visit to the school and introducing the idea of guide dogs. Morris Frank, an individual who was blind, heard about her experience with guide dogs and contacted Ms. Eutis to inquire about obtaining a guide dog to provide him with independence. Ms. Eutis trained Buddy, a female German Shepherd, for Mr. Frank. In return, Mr. Frank worked to establish the first dog guide

*He is your friend, your partner, your defender, your dog. You are his life, his love, his leader. He will be yours, faithful and true to the last beat of his heart. You owe it to him to be worthy of such devotion.*
*- Unknown*

*Patch, a hearing dog, alerts her owner to the sound of the telephone ringing. Patch's orange vest identifies her as a professionally trained hearing dog. Photo courtesy of International Hearing Dogs, Inc.*

school in Nashville, Tennessee. Incorporated on January 29, 1929, it was called The Seeing Eye.

The idea of working dogs coming to the aid of individuals with physical disabilities other than blindness has been attributed to Dr. Bonnie Bergin. In 1974 while on travel in Turkey, Dr. Bergin observed an individual with paralysis using a donkey to assist him with transportation. Based on this symbiotic partnership, Dr. Bergin developed tasks and associated command structures for dogs to provide service to individuals with disabilities. Thus was born the concept of the "service dog." Dr. Bergin's efforts were the first to expand the training of a dog to provide the broad set of physical skills necessary to meet the needs of individuals with varied disabilities. Dr. Bergin made the initial recog-

nition of teamwork between human and dog, which would lead to the enablement of individuals with disabilities to function with greater self-sufficiency, to prevent injuries, to become aware of events in the environment, and to summon help in a crisis.

The early utilization of assistance dogs and the eventual social acceptance that assistance dogs are not pets has led to their inclusion in United States federal law under the Americans with Disabilities Act of 1990 (ADA). Legally the ADA defines an assistance dog as ". . . any dog that has been individually trained to provide assistance or perform tasks for the benefit of a person with a physical or mental disability, substantially limiting one or more major life functions." In some states, the definition of an assistance dog has been expanded to include any dog trained or being trained by a recognized school for training dogs to assist persons with disabilities. This federal protection has been expanded to protect the rights of individuals with disabilities to be accompanied by their assistance dogs in public places, i.e., businesses, restaurants, theaters, hotels, public schools and nearly anyplace open to the general public. Assistance dogs are permitted to ride public transportation, such as taxicabs, buses, trains and airplanes.

As with many laws and regulations, the confusion over legal definitions and the existence of legal loopholes is also true of laws regarding service animals. Some individuals interpret the regulatory language on service animals for selfish purposes ignoring the ADA training requirements. To address this and other issues which could negatively impact the preservation of access rights under the

ADA, the Coalition of Assistance Dog Organizations (CADO) was formed in 2001 by the alliance of the Guide Dog Users, Inc., the International Association of Assistance Dog Partners, the National Association of Guide Dog Users, Assistance Dogs International, and the U.S. Council of Dog Guide Schools. CADO continues to advocate the use of "task training" as the legal litmus test of service animal legitimacy by the U.S. Department of Justice. CADO sees this test necessary to distinguish between people with disabilities who work with a service animal to mitigate their disabling condition and those who are participating in pet based mental health or physical health facilitation with a pet dog, reptile or any other species of animal.

In 2003, CADO members proposed the following updated terminology to be utilized as the definition of Service Animal in the ADA (28 CFR 36.104) and in communications with the U.S. Department of Justice and other government agencies:

> Service animal means an assistance dog, and may include other animals specifically trained to perform physical tasks to mitigate an individual's disability. Assistance dogs include: guide dogs that guide individuals who are legally blind; hearing dogs that alert individuals who are deaf or hard of hearing to specific sounds; and service dogs for individuals with disabilities other than blindness or deafness. Service dogs are trained to perform a variety of physical tasks, including but not limited to pulling a wheelchair, lending balance support, picking up dropped objects or providing assistance in a medical crisis. The presence of an animal for comfort, protection or personal defense does not qualify an animal as being trained to mitigate an individual's disability and therefore does not qualify said animal as a service animal.

Although this definition enjoys widespread support among disability advocates, it is yet to be legislated into law. This definition may seem a bit confusing and circular, as is true with most legalease; however, it remains necessary to make these distinctions as they preserve the historic terminology of the service animal industry and agree with commonly used language.

## ASSISTANCE DOG RECIPIENTS

It is estimated that over 20,000 people with disabilities in the United States use assistance dogs. For many individuals these disabilities are invisible. Therefore, every person who is accompanied by an assistance dog may or may not "look" disabled, and under the ADA an assistance dog is not required to have any special certification.

Assistance dogs have historically been used by individuals with mobility limitations such as blindness, paraplegia, quadriplegia, and individuals who utilize assistive devices, for example, canes or walkers. However, the task training has been expanded to enable assistance dogs to serve individuals with a variety of diagnoses including, but not limited to, hearing loss, spinal cord injury, brain injury, stroke, visual or hearing impairments, arthritis, ataxia, multiple sclerosis, cerebral palsy, muscular dystrophy, spina bifida, seizure disorders, cardio-pulmonary disease, arterio-vascular disease, diabetes, and psychiatric disabilities.

The most common types of assistance dogs are guide dogs, service dogs, hearing alert dogs, and seizure alert/seizure response dogs. These dogs perform many tasks, some of which may include:

- **Guide Dog or Dog Guide** – Assist people with vision loss, lead these individuals around physical obstacles and to destinations such as seating, crossing streets, entering or exiting doorways, elevators and stairways, etc.
- **Service Dog** – Retrieve and carry items, open doors and drawers, push buttons; Assist people with mobility limitations to walk, balance, dress, transfer from place to place; pull wheelchair, and aid with household chores such as putting in and removing clothes from washer/dryer.
- **Hearing Alert Dog** – Alert people with a hearing loss to the presence of specific sounds, such as doorbells, telephones, crying babies, sirens, another person, buzzing timers or sensors, knocks at a door, and smoke, fire, or clock alarms.
- **Seizure Alert/Seizure Response Dog** – Alerts or responds to medical conditions, such as heart attack, stroke, diabetes, epilepsy, panic attack, anxiety attack, post-traumatic stress, and seizures. According to Lynn Hoekstra, Regional Director, Paws With A Cause, Seizure Dogs can be described as "alerting" (which some people think means they will *predict*) or "responding" (the seizure is the cue which causes the dog to react and do the task they were trained to do). Paws believes they can train a dog to respond (i.e., pull emergency cord, retrieve phone, lick person's face, etc.) and some dogs will eventually start to show some predicting behaviors (becoming restless, pushing against the person to protect them, etc.). Some dogs will do a wonderful job responding to seizures, but never develop the ability to predict. That does not lessen the help they give by responding as they were trained to do.

*Courtesy of Assistance Dogs of the West.*

Not every person who is accompanied by an assistance dog looks disabled. Assistance dogs also assist individuals with hearing loss, seizure disorders, diabetes, and other disabilities.

In addition to these federally recognized assistance dogs identified above, there are other types of dogs that provide services to individuals with disabilities that do not have federal legal status. Therapy dogs, typically referred to as pets, are dogs that provide emotional service only. Therapy Dogs International, Inc. (http://www.tdi-dog) certifies all types of dog breeds for the purpose of visiting nursing homes, hospitals, or other institutions, and wherever else therapy dogs are needed. Therapy dogs provide emotional support and are not trained to perform specific tasks.

## THE MAKING OF AN ASSISTANCE DOG

Creating an assistance dog is a labor intensive and lengthy process. Some people choose to "owner-train" their assistance dog. Training your own assistance dog is a complex undertaking that depends on your lifestyle and dog knowledge. This book addresses dogs trained through an organization according to the standards established by the Assistance Dogs International. The training process begins with the identification of a candidate puppy that can come from a variety of places, including, but not limited to, breeders, donating families, or animal shelters. Determining whether a puppy is capable of becoming an assistance dog is based on several factors. The initial step in the identification of a candidate puppy is the determination whether or not the puppy has the right temperament. He or she should be calm and friendly, but focused and not easily distracted. Overly dominant puppies may develop aggressions toward people or other animals over time. Labradors, Golden Retrievers, and German Shepherds are breeds recognized for their good temperament and tendency toward assistance work; however, other working breeds such as the Standard Poodle, Welsh Corgi, Shetland Sheepdog, and a variety of other full and mixed breeds make excellent assistance dogs.

Once a candidate puppy is identified, it is placed with a puppy raiser or foster family (please see Chapter 11) for up to eighteen months to form the initial human-canine bonding experiences. These volunteers socialize the puppy, exposing him or her to different kinds of social situations and stressful environments such as office settings, public transportation, and large crowds. They also provide basic obedience training. These activities and situations will help

> Potential Service Dogs are selected as puppies on the basis of temperament and ability to focus.

*Courtesy of Assistance Dogs of the West.*

> Volunteer puppy raisers socialize the puppy and provide basic obedience training.

prepare the puppy for the services he or she will one day be required to perform in public environments. The puppy raiser or foster family is often financially responsible for the puppy, covering both daily care and veterinary expenses.

The next phase is the training of a puppy and can begin anywhere from 12 months to 2 years of age. This phase of training is conducted by a professional trainer employed by the assistance dog agency and involves reinforcing basic obedience and social skills, positive reinforcement for desired behavior, and verbal reprimands for inappropriate behavior.

Sometimes puppies live in the trainer's home to become acclimated to the everyday routines of a household and to further develop human-canine bonding. During this phase of training, the young

*"Denver Dog" alerts Mom to the cries of her baby. Courtesy of International Hearing Dogs Inc.*

## Service Dog Commands

The following is a list of commands that my Golden Retriever, Paws With A Cause service dog, Morgan, is trained to perform. This is the language he and I use to communicate with each other. When Morgan and I were paired, he already knew this language and I had to learn how to speak the commands so that Morgan would respond to me and perform the tasks that would help me be more independent:

**Dog's Name** – Is used to get the dog's attention and let him know to whom you are speaking. It is also used to call the dog.
**Heel** – Tells the dog to go to your left side.
**Sit** – Tells the dog to sit.
**Down** – Tells the dog to lie down (this does not mean off).
**Come** – Calls the dog to you, but not in any special position.
**Sit–Stay** – Tells the dog to sit and to stay in his current position.
**Down-Stay** – Tells the dog to lie down and to stay in his current position.
**Side** – Tells the dog to go to your right side.
**No** – Tells the dog to stop whatever he is doing.
**Stand** – Tells the dog to stand on all four feet.
**Wait** – Prevents the dog from crossing a barrier or threshold. It is also used to have the dog turn and wait after the go-through.

**Follow** – Tells the dog to follow behind you through a doorway or narrow passage.

**Give** – Tells the dog to release the object in his mouth.

**Drop It** – Tells the dog to drop the item he has in his mouth.

**Kennel** – Tells the dog to go into his kennel, bed, crate, or vehicle.

**Up** – Tells the dog to put his paws on the wall, counter, or some other object.

**Step** – Is used with walking brace dogs to tell the dog to go to the next step.

**Switch** – Tells the dog to push the light switch up with his nose to turn on or to use his mouth to turn the light off.

**Move** – Tells the dog to pull the wheelchair.

**Back** – Tells the dog to step backwards, usually after a go-through.

**Lap** – Tells the dog to put his front paws on your lap.

**Off** – Tells the dog to get off something or someone.

**Under** – Tells the dog to crawl under a table, desk, or other small space to lie down. Usually followed by a stay.

**Take-It** – Tells the dog to pick-up something.

**Bring** – Tells the dog to bring the object to you.

**Hold** – Tells the dog to hold on to whatever you have asked him to retrieve for you.

**Right** – Tells the dog to turn right.

**Left** – Tells the dog to turn left.

**Easy** – Tells the dog to slow down or be gentle.

**Stop** – Tells the dog to stop pulling the wheelchair. Also in an emergency situation at a distance, dog must stop and stay.

**Up-Take-It** – Tells the dog to put his front paws on a counter or something and pick up an item.

**Up-Give** – Tells the dog to puts his front paws on a counter and drop an item, or hand an item to the person giving the command.

**Get Help** – Tells the dog to go find someone and paw them because you need help, and then to lead the person back to you.

**Go-Out/Stay** – Tells the dog to pull open a heavy commercial door for you. Stay will then tell him to hold the door open so you can position your wheelchair to block the door open so you can enter.

**Phone** – Tells the dog to get the phone and bring it back to you.

**Door** – Tells the dog to open or close an interior door.

**Fridge** – Tells the dog to open the refrigerator door.

**Close-It** – Tells the dog to close the refrigerator.

**Pull** – Tells the dog to pull the emergency cord.

**Paw** – Tells the dog to jump up with his paw on the wall and push an elevator button, push plate or door bell. Also, to alert the client with one paw.

**Harness** – Tells the dog to put his head through the backpack harness.

**Leave-It** – Tells the dog to stop paying attention outwardly and turn his attention back on the person or task they were doing.

**About** – Tells the dog to turn around in a heel position so the other side of his pack can be clipped.

**Around** – 1) Used when the dog is in a Flexi leash and goes behind the chair on the opposite side. 2) Tells the dog to go behind the chair to the opposite side.

**Take-A-Break** – Tells the dog to eliminate on or off leash.

**Watch-Me** – Tells the dog to look at you after his name has been said.

**Settle** – Tells the dog to calm down.

**Free** – Tells the dog he is released from any command.

**Open** – Tells the dog to back-up and hold the door open until he is released. For dogs that open a commercial door with their mouth.

**Chair** – To pull a manual wheelchair to the client when they are away from the wheelchair (for a short distance only).

**Lift** – Tells the dog to lift an arm, head, torso or legs.

**Try Again** – Used after the dog has tried to do a command, but fails.

**Quiet** – Tells the dog to silence barking or whining.

**Take-It/Bring** – Tells the dog to pull the bed covers up over the client.

**Take-It/Back** – Tells the dog to pull the bed covers back off of the client.

dogs continue to undergo health screenings, temperament evaluation, and trainability testing, which may include retrieving and wheelchair pulling.

The training of an assistance dog then progresses to the assistance dog agency's advanced training phase which usually occurs at the agency's headquarters or training facility. At this time, the young dog is taught the specific tasks and commands necessary to respond to specific disability-related needs, which will vary depending upon the dog's physical and mental abilities. These tasks may include:

- *Guide Dog Tasks* – a set of tasks allowing an individual with vision loss to negotiate the unseen environment with safety and independence. These tasks or duties can be grouped into three primary skill categories: obstacle avoidance, signaling changes in elevation, and locating objects.
- *Hearing Dog Tasks* – a set of tasks alerting an individual with hearing loss to specific sounds, including obedience and public access manners. These tasks are grouped into two primary skill categories: alerting to specific sounds and other possible tasks.
- *Service Dog Tasks* – a set of tasks involving general obedience, public access manners, and assistance to people who have a wide variety of mobility limitations, which could allow such individuals to conserve energy, reduce or avoid pain, minimize dependency on loved ones, prevent injuries, or get help in a crisis. These tasks can be grouped into the following skill categories: retrieval-based tasks, carrying-based tasks, deposit-based tasks, tug-based

tasks, nose-nudge-based tasks, pawing-based tasks, bracing-based tasks, harness-based tasks, and other kinds of assistance in crisis including medical assistance tasks.

- *Medical Alert or Response Dog Tasks* – a set of tasks useful to individuals with hidden disabilities, such as seizure disorders, psychiatric disorders, a potentially life threatening medical problem, or conditions of chronic pain.

After completing Advanced Training the assistance dog is prepared for placement and will begin Team Training with a qualified recipient. Compatibility between the recipient and assistance dog is extremely important, and the lifestyle of the recipient must be considered when choosing the appropriate assistance dog partner. Team Training may involve both group lessons and individualized instruction where the recipient learns the commands for the tasks that his dog will be performing in order to effectively assist him. Careful attention is paid by the trainer to determine if the necessary partnership between the service dog and the recipient is developing. Team Training can last from two weeks to two months depending on the assistance dog provider agency. Once the team has completed Team Training, the agencies provide a variation of staff follow-up visits and consultations. During these visits, staff will monitor the working team's progress. These visits become less frequent as the team builds experience and confidence in each other.

Most agencies provide a laminated identification card that states the assistance dog and the recipient's names and shows a picture of the dog. The working team may be required to take public access and/or periodic recertification tests, which indicate the team's ability to function in public. It is customary for the dogs to wear a harness or backpack displaying a logo that identifies them as assistance dogs.

## BEHAVIOR AND TRAINING STANDARDS

Assistance Dogs International, Inc. (http://www.adionline.org) publishes minimum standards for assistance dog training programs to ensure the highest level of performance, behavior, and quality in training and assistance dog performance.

### Behavior and Training Standards for All Service Animals

For over 75 years, assistance dogs have worked successfully in public and won the public's acceptance by achieving high behavioral and training standards, which set them apart from pets and other animals. In order to assure the comfort and safety of people with disabilities and the general public, high behavioral and training standards must apply equally to all service animals. ADI believes that all service animals intended for use in public, regardless of species, should be required to meet the same standards required of dogs specifically trained to assist people with disabilities. Any animal that can meet the existing standards for behavior, training, cleanliness, and public appropriateness should be allowed to work in public when accompanied by the person for whose disability it was specifically trained. These standards include:

*Kevin and Service Dog Elya Gerri. Photo Courtesy of Alicia Chatman.*

### Public Appropriateness:
- Animal is clean and does not have a foul odor.
- Animal does not urinate or defecate in inappropriate locations.

### Behavior:
- Animal does not annoy any member of the general public.
- Animal's conduct does not disrupt the normal course of business.
- Animal works without unnecessary vocalization.
- Animal shows no aggression toward people or other animals.
- Animal does not solicit or steal food or other items from the general public.

# CHAPTER TWO
## Making the Decision to Get a Service Dog

Years ago, I was flipping through the television channels during the afternoon and landed on the local Public Broadcasting Service airing of a documentary on service dogs. On the screen was a yellow Labrador Retriever opening the refrigerator for a young man who was paralyzed and used a wheelchair. My husband, Franz, and I sat in amazement both sharing the same thought and desire. We had to get one of those. As a twenty-something year old woman in a wheelchair, it sounded like a good idea to have a dog with me that could be of assistance and offer me peace of mind. After that moment and for over a year afterward, I thought about what it would mean to have a dog in my life 24 hours a day, 7 days a week. Franz and I had many discussions about the subject and both felt it was something I should pursue. I sought out more specific information about service dogs to discover what a dog could do for me.

At the time of the documentary airing I had written down the agency's name: Canine Companions for Independence. I called directory assistance and contacted Canine Companions for an information packet. When it arrived in the mail, my heart was pounding with excitement. This was my first step toward having my own service dog. As I mentioned, the dog in the documentary was yellow, so jokingly Franz and I began referring to my potential service dog as "Yellow Dog".

As we read through the information packet, I realized that I fit this agency's recipient criteria perfectly. However, I found later that every agency has different eligibility criteria for service dog recipients and different policies governing service dog partnerships. I investigated other agencies and found that some of them charged a fee for a service dog, while others provided a dog at no cost. Some agencies had training facilities and required recipients to participate in an onsite training program, while others sent a dog and trainer directly to the recipient's home. Although not an issue for me, age is a factor as some agencies may not place a dog with a child under the age of 18. Some agencies turn ownership of the dog over to the recipient, while other agencies maintain ownership. Little did I realize at the time that this ownership policy would have major implications during my first service dog, Ramona's, retirement and affect my decision regarding her successor dog.

The common thread among all the agencies I reviewed was the expectation

*"Until one has loved an animal a part of one's soul remains unawakened."*
*- Anatole France*

*Donna Hebel uses her assistance dog to provide stability. Photo Courtesy of Alicia Chatman.*

## Are You Eligible For A Service Dog?

Each service dog agency has different eligibility requirements for service dog recipients. Be prepared to answer some personal questions about yourself, your disability, and your personal finances. Some of the common eligibility requirements or considerations are:

- Proof of disability from doctor or disability provider;
- Recipient's age is an eligibility requirement for some agencies that require recipients to be legal adults while other agencies will accommodate and even specialize in providing service dogs to children under certain parameters.
- Participation in a personal interview;
- Completion of a written application;
- Resources and ability to travel to and stay at a training facility;
- Resources and ability to care for and support the service dog (i.e., space, food, veterinary care, etc.);

Keep in mind, if you are not eligible under one program's guidelines, you may be eligible under another. For example, service dog agencies have individual eligibility requirements such as mobility, levels of physical strength, etc. Some service dog agencies also provide the dog free of charge while others require a monetary fee.

that recipients make a long term commitment to their service dog. This commitment is two-fold. Recipients must be willing to assume the monetary responsibility of day-to-day care and maintenance of their service dog which includes feeding, watering, grooming, vet care, etc. Consider your willingness to have a dog at your side 24 hours a day, 7 days a week, even sleeping in or by your bed at night. Just as important is the commitment to the ongoing growth of the relationship which is like any solid relationship and includes working and playing together and investing the time and energy necessary to build and maintain a healthy working team.

The ultimate question you have to ask yourself when considering getting a service dog is, "Will having a service dog enable me to be more independent?" If the answer is yes, here are some additional questions to consider:

- Can I physically handle a dog?

- Can I care for the dog or can I figure out alternative care through an attendant, family member, or caregiver?
- Can I afford to take care of a dog, i.e., vet care, grooming, food, medication?
- Can my house accommodate a dog? If I live in an apartment, where would I toilet my dog and could I clean up after my dog?
- If I have pets, how would they respond to a trained dog?
- If I have children, how would they react to a dog?
- Is my spouse or significant other supportive of me getting a dog?
- What type of transportation would my dog and I utilize and how will that impact my daily routine?
- How does my employer feel about me getting a dog?
- How will getting a dog impact my house and household? If I rent, how should I approach my landlord?

## HOW TO APPLY FOR A SERVICE DOG

As you begin the application process, it is recommended that you become familiar with the agencies that set the standards for the assistance dog industry, Assistance Dogs International, Inc. (ADI) and the International Association of Assistance Dog Partners (IAADP). "ADI is a coalition of nonprofit organizations that train and place assistance dogs. The purpose of ADI is to improve the areas of training, placement, and utilization of Assistance Dogs as well as staff and volunteer education" (Retrieved from www.adionline.org). ADI provides valuable information including a member list and links to ser-

**Recipients must be willing to make a long-term commitment to take responsibility for their service dog.**

vice dog agencies. IAADP is "a nonprofit, cross-disability organization representing people partnered with guide, hearing, and service dogs" whose mission is "to provide assistance dog partners with a voice in the assistance dog field; enable those partnered with guide dogs, hearing dogs and service dogs to work together on issues of mutual concern; and to foster the disabled person/assistance dog partnership" (Retrieved from www.iaadp.org).

According to their website, "The Delta Society is a leading international resource for the human-animal bond…" and "…has been the force to validate the important role of animals for people's health and well-being…" since 1977. The Delta Society's primary mission is to improve human health and well-being through service and therapy animals. The Delta Society was the first organization to provide credible research on why animals are important to the general population and more specifically how they affect health and well-being. In the 1990s, the Delta Society developed the Standards of Practice in Animal-Assisted Activities and Animal-Assisted Therapy which provided guidance regarding animal selection, personnel training, treatment plan development, documentation, etc. The Delta Society's website contains helpful information regarding frequently asked questions, basic information about service dogs, the type of individuals service dogs

## Important Questions to Ask a Potential Service Dog Agency

The application process is an intensely personal experience, and it is important for you to select a service dog agency carefully. To assist those of you seeking your first service dog, we have compiled some basic questions you should ask a service dog agency or representative:

- What types of tasks are the dogs trained to perform and how will I be matched with a service dog?
- How long is the waiting list or waiting period?
- What is the cost associated with the dog?
- Can I have another animal in the house (i.e., pets such as dogs, cats, birds, etc.)?
- Does the initial training occur at your facility or in my home? And if so, what costs are associated with either training location?
- Once a dog is placed with me, what level of after-care and follow-up is provided including any form of re-certification or additional training?
- Once a dog is placed with me, will I own the dog or will the agency maintain ownership?
- What happens when it is time for my dog to retire?
- What is the process for getting a successor dog?

can help, consumer information for people considering a service dog, and other information regarding the service dog education system.

Both Assistance Dogs International and The Delta Society have a comprehensive list of registered organizations that provide working dogs to individuals with disabilities, and a list of service dog trainers and training programs throughout the United States and abroad. For a list of current service dog trainers and training programs provided by the Delta Society please refer to the Resource section.

After careful consideration and research, I elected to apply to Canine Companions for Independence because they best met my needs at that time. I was paralyzed from the waist down with full use of my arms so I could handle a dog. I was over 18 and financially able to care for a dog. My husband supported the idea 200 percent. I had been depending completely on him to take me to work and to any other activity such as shopping or one of my volunteer commitments. At that time I could use hand controls to drive, but I had fallen many times and felt insecure being alone in a parking lot or in public places. Based on my research and discoveries of the wonderful possibilities of having a service dog, it was settled that I would apply. As we were going through the application we read one statement that made our hearts sink. The fine print stated that there was a potential four year waiting list. We were in shock. Four years! How could I have wasted one whole year just considering the idea?

As the shock wore off, I vigilantly began preparing the application and what an application it was. I had to consult with doctors, therapists, and other professionals in order to provide the information that was requested. After completing and submitting my written application, I was scheduled for a telephone interview with the Executive Director of the program in my area. Later, during that interview, she quickly confirmed that I would be an excellent candidate and congratulated me for officially earning a spot on the waiting list for a service dog. The list, the list, that dreaded list that stood between me and my new canine partner. I began examining my future plans and wondered how the pieces would come together.

One Sunday afternoon, as fate would have it, Franz and I went to the local mall. As we were making our way through the

*Kings Valley Collies, © Eva Rappaport.*

Applicants for service dogs go through rigorous interviews and waiting lists can seem very long; however, most agencies are working diligently to reduce applicant's waiting time.

mall, we heard a dog barking. There was an animal fair going on and we saw dogs wearing capes. I looked at Franz and said, "Yellow Dog!" We rushed toward the barking, turned the corner, and our eyes almost popped out of our head as we saw a table draped with a "Canine Companions for Independence" banner. Sitting at the table were several adults and the most beautiful dogs dressed in "puppy-in-training" capes that we had ever seen. We quickly introduced ourselves and proudly shared with them the fact that I was on the waiting list for a service dog. Dot and Jim, Patty and Jeff were the normal, every–day people who were changing other's lives by training these remarkable animals and then selflessly giving them up to someone with a disability. They were delighted to hear I lived in Tallahassee and had been officially accepted as a candidate because at that time there were

no service dogs in Tallahassee. These wonderful people had already raised several dogs and were well versed in the service dog arena. We were elated! Immediately, they became our new family and began educating us about the service dog world. They invited us to come to the puppy classes where they were training future service dogs and into their homes where we visited with them and learned of their expertise and dedication.

Franz and I could not believe we had moved into the service dog world so quickly and that we had developed such a great relationship with these wonderful people. They became as interested as we were in the "infamous" waiting list and where I was in line for my new partner. As the days, weeks, and months passed by, Franz and I accepted every invitation our new found friends offered to visit with them and even to baby sit the puppies if they needed to go out of town. We looked for any excuse to spend time with them and their puppies.

I was at work one afternoon when I received the call which would change my life. It was Ellen with Canine Companions for Independence in Farmington, New York, calling to invite me to their fall team training and wondering if I was still interested in receiving a service dog. I could not believe it was finally happening and told her that I was definitely still interested. I shrieked with excitement and my coworkers ran to my office to see what was happening. Ellen went on to give me various details on which I could hardly concentrate. I could not believe that the time had finally arrived when my dream and my goal were finally coming true. I assured Ellen I would accept the spot in the class, hung up the phone and immediately called Franz. We then called our new puppy raising friends, Dot, Jim, Patty, and Jeff, to share our jubilation. As Franz and I got home that evening we began talking about the details for my trip,

which included airfare to New York, an accessible rental van for two weeks, hotel expenses for two weeks, food, etc. The more we talked, the more overwhelming these details became, but somehow we would come up with the money. We had to.

The next day, Dot called me at work and announced that they (Dot, Jim, Patty, and Jeff) were paying for my travel expenses and they did not want to hear any objections. My jaw dropped and tears filled my eyes. I immediately began to respond with, "But, but, but," and she said, "No 'buts,' that's it." I cannot begin to describe how incredibly blessed Franz and I felt. We were overwhelmed with emotion and joy. Dot took it upon herself to make the arrangements for our trip to New York. Franz and I would fly up together on Saturday, he would get me settled in the hotel on Sunday, go with me to my first day of training on Monday, and then return to Tallahassee leaving me alone for the training. Then Dot and Jim would drive to New York at the end of the training and bring Franz along for my graduation. Dot was very busy making all of the arrangements. She and Jim contacted a recipient of one of their puppies who was an agent for Wheelchair Getaways, a rental company that specialized in accessible van rentals. They secured an accessible van for me at no cost for the entire two week period.

Whew! We were in shock. How could these people be so wonderful? This could not be happening, but it was. Dot and Jim, Patty and Jeff, along with their puppies in training, Annie and Panama, came to our apartment early that Saturday morning and escorted us to the airport for a wonderful send off. They were still waving and taking pictures as I was wheeled down the jetway.

*Service dog Gerri opens an office door for his owner, Kevin Elya. Photo Courtesy of Alicia Chatman.*

# CHAPTER THREE
## They Don't Call it Boot Camp for Nothing

I was so nervous and anxious to arrive at Team Training. What would my dog's name be? Would it be a female or a male? Would he or she like me? I figured they would like Franz more than me. He would be able to run and play with the dog. I would be the gimp making him or her work. All of these things flew through my head as we made our way to New York. When we arrived at La Guardia, Dot and Jim's friend Rick, his wife, and his service dog, Hester, met us at the airport and escorted us to the beautiful conversion van that was awaiting our arrival. They even followed us to the hotel and took us to dinner that evening. I, of course, was asking every question I could think of about Team Training. As we sat in the restaurant, I looked down at his wheelchair to see a little yellow head resting on his footplate with big brown eyes looking up at him in awe. My heart started beating like crazy again. Would I ever have a dog look at me like that?

Franz and I spent Sunday preparing my room for his departure. He moved the furniture around to accommodate my wheelchair. He called maintenance to come in and add an extra grab bar to assist me in safely getting out of the bathtub. He thought of everything that could be a potential barrier. We spent that afternoon exploring Long Island and talking about Yellow Dog. I was very anxious about Franz leaving me there alone. I would have to drive myself to the training center every morning in rush hour traffic. I would have to eat alone. And, most of all, I would be alone with my new service dog. Could I handle it?

Monday morning finally came. Franz and I made our way to the training center. I was excited and nervous. We entered the facility and were escorted into a room with other people in wheelchairs. I sat nervously clinging to Franz as the staff entered and began talking to us about team training. They informed us that every morning we would have an exam. This would not be a multiple choice exam, but an essay exam about the commands and other pertinent information we needed to know about our dogs, such as grooming, cleanliness, and other responsibilities. We were reminded that these animals were not robots and it was going to take hard work and motivation to get them to work for us. It became very apparent that this was going to be a difficult and rigid program, but in the end I would have a new life partner.

After the introductions and the "dos" and "don'ts," the trainers opened the

*The trainer said as she slipped the leash tightly around my wrist, "This is Ramona," a sleek, black Labrador/Golden Retriever mix. "She is wonderful." I looked down and whispered, "You're the one." Thus, began my journey of independence with a service dog.*
*– Marcie Davis*

doors and what seemed like hundreds of dogs poured into the room. They ran from one end of the room to the other sniffing our wheelchairs and practically everything else. Some of them jumped on us as they moved freely around the room. The trainers just stood back and watched and then, just as quickly as they entered the room, the dogs were shuffled out. Wow, just think, one of those animals was going to be my new service dog. I could hardly stand the anticipation. Which one would it be?

As the first day went on, the trainers brought in various dogs for each participant. We rolled our wheelchairs around in a circle with our dogs as they taught us our basic first command—how to "heel." The trainers were watching our every move and evaluating our performance with each dog. As the first day came to a close, I was saddened by the thought that Franz was leaving me to return home. But, I knew I needed to face this challenge on my own, and as much as Franz loved and supported me, he had to go home. As Tuesday morning came, Franz helped me get dressed and went with me to the training facility for the first hour of class. He slipped out of the training room as I was going around in a circle with this strange new creature. He was gone and I was on my own. I was by myself, 1,200 miles from the security of my husband and all the things that were familiar to me. I was alone in a hotel room on a quest for independence.

On the second day, we were asked to write down the names of the dogs that were our first, second, and third choices. A fellow participant leaned over to me and said, "If you put down Rochester as your first choice, I'll have to kill you."

Rochester was a shiny black Lab that I had considered one of my top three, but to honor my new friend's wishes, I omitted him from my list. Newton was my first choice, an energetic Golden Retriever. I felt a connection with him because his name was Newton, as in Sir Isaac Newton, and Franz was studying to be a physicist. To my delight, the trainer presented me with Newton, and I worked with him all day.

On the third day, we took our new dogs back to our hotel with us. From then on, the dogs were supposed to stay with us 24 hours a day. I loaded Newton into my van and escorted him back to the hotel. Everything was going fine until we entered the hotel elevator that was lined with mirrors. Newton became very nervous, which made me very nervous.

At the training center the next morning I knew I had to tell Ellen, the head trainer, about Newton's elevator reaction. As soon as we arrived, the trainers began questioning us about our dog's performance at the hotel. When I shared Newton's reaction, he was immediately whisked away and I could hear the trainers whispering and conspiring.

When they reappeared, they brought Patty to me. She was a large, stoic, yellow Labrador Retriever. As Patty and I worked together, she performed beautifully. The only problem with Patty was her nonstop drooling. Streams of saliva hung from her mouth as she stoically performed each command. Ellen looked at me and asked "What's wrong?" She felt that Patty and I were working together perfectly, but we did not seem happy together. I confessed to her that I worked in an office environment and I was concerned about

Agencies make special efforts to match the service dog with the recipient's needs and lifestyle. It may take several tries before the right partner is found.

Patty's overactive drooling. Patty's leash was taken off my wrist and once again I sat with no dog.

"What's wrong with me?" I thought as I looked around the room at my classmates bonding with their new dogs. The day ended and I returned to the hotel alone. I felt like a failure and wondered if I had come over a thousand miles from home for nothing.

The next day when I returned to the training center I was presented with another yellow Labrador, Nancy. My heart skipped a beat because I knew Nancy. Nancy had been raised by our dear friends Dot and Jim. I knew Dot secretly wanted me to get Nancy, but I also knew the trainers would kill me if I did not confess that I had a close friendship with Nancy's puppy raisers. I confessed to Ellen and, as predicted, she took Nancy's leash off my wrist and she was gone.

We went outside for a group photo and I was the only one in the class without a dog. Almost the entire first week of training was over and I sat alone watching the rest of my classmates with their new companions. As I sat there, tears were welling up in my eyes and I was developing a feeling of failure. About that time, Ellen came from behind me. As I turned to look at her, she took a leash and clasped it tightly around my wrist. She said, "This is Ramona." Ramona was a beautiful, sleek,

*Assistance dogs in training. Courtesy of Assistance Dogs of the West.*

black Labrador/Golden Retriever mix. I looked down at her and my tears turned to joy. I whispered to Ramona, "You're the one." I felt such a feeling of peace as Ramona's tail wagged uncontrollably. She was the one, and we were beginning a new journey together. I quickly made my way to the group preparing for the photo and smiled as widely and proudly as I could. I now had a service dog and I was ready to begin my new life with her.

We trained earnestly together. Ramona knew all of the commands. It was my job to learn how to communicate with her and demonstrate our proficiency as a working team. She was

## Service Dog Placement

As you can see from my story, matching a recipient with a service dog is not an exact science. Trainers must consider a host of factors when creating a service dog team. Temperament and personality of both the individual and the dog are taken into serious consideration. The first dog selected is not always the dog that will become your service dog. Be prepared and be flexible to endure the selection process. Trust me; it is worth it to be sure that you have the dog most compatible with you and your physical needs.

trained in over 50 commands that would enable her to pick up things that I dropped, open doors, including the refrigerator, bark on command, pull my wheelchair, and a host of other physical things that would make life easier for me. Barking on command was one of the hardest things to get a dog to do. I was so thrilled when I instructed Ramona to "Speak," and she bellowed out the loudest bark. I was so proud. I knew she was happy being with me. Every time when we went in for the night, she would dive onto the bed and run around in circles until her tongue hung out. Then she would collapse and look at me with those beautiful brown eyes as if to say, "It's just me and you, girlfriend!" Maybe she just liked sleeping in bed. I did not care. I just enjoyed seeing her so happy and knowing that she was my new companion.

Every training program has its positive aspects as well as demands. Guide Dogs for the Blind have training centers in San Rafael, California, and Boring, Oregon, where recipients attend training and are later matched with their dogs. Airfare is paid for and recipients are provided with accommodations and gourmet meals on beautiful campuses at no cost; however, the expectations of every participant are high. Training days are long and grueling, leaving recipients emotionally drained. The first day is spent getting oriented to the facility and its surroundings. The following two and a half days are filled with workouts in which the instructor simulates a guide dog in a harness to get a sense of the recipient's pace and footwork in order to select the most compatible dog. Then comes "Dog Day" when private individual introductions are conducted. Over the remainder of the training period the teams adhere to a strict schedule of lectures and workouts where they learn how to care for their dogs and navigate different environments and obstacles, such as, streets, curbs, escalators, and elevators. As the teams gain confidence working together, the tasks become more complex and the instructor becomes more passive, allowing the team to work together as an independent unit. Shelly Ondich, a guide dog recipient says, "By the time you finish, you really feel like you've accomplished something!" She described the experience as wonderful, taking place in a positive environment that helped her survive those difficult training days when she thought "I can't handle this." The training culminated with a final "task" that she described as an exhilarating hike in the woods, which is conducted shortly before the graduation ceremony. Like some assistance dog agencies, Guide Dogs for the Blind sends a field representative to conduct an in-home recertification of the team around the one year anniversary date of the team's graduation. Subsequent follow up is usually done over the telephone until the guide dog is nearing retirement; at that point, an in-home assessment is necessary to assess the dog's ability to work and to plan for the possibility of a successor dog.

## MONITORING THE TEAM'S SUCCESS

As training was coming to a close, I was anxiously awaiting Franz's return for graduation. I had missed him terribly and could not wait for him to meet Ramona. I knew they were going to love each other as much as I loved both of them. But I was sad and a little frightened to think about leaving the training center. It was so safe there with our trainers always available to help us. What was I going to do when I went out into the world by myself? Was I ready? Was Ramona ready?

Franz finally arrived Friday, and graduation was on Saturday night. I'll never forget waiting for him in the hotel lobby with Ramona. She sat by my side as he approached us. He smiled uncontrollably as he walked toward us. Based on explicit instructions from the trainers, Franz knew that he could not talk to or touch Ramona. He was not allowed to have any interaction with her for the first month of our partnership.

Ramona and I had to complete one last hurdle before graduation—the public access test. In order to pass this test, Ramona had to purchase an item for me in a store, navigate narrow aisles, and retrieve a dropped object in a crowded mall. We passed with flying colors, but

*Marcie and Ramona complete CCI Team Training and become a working service dog team.*

*Two generations of service dogs, Canine Companion for Independence service dog in training, Janice IV, and Paws With A Cause service dog, Morgan. Photograph courtesy of Franz Freibert.*

our journey was really just beginning. A working dog team is an ongoing relationship that requires follow-up training and, in some cases, recertification. The trainers reminded us that they were available to talk with us in case an issue arose after graduation.

Graduation was a night I will never forget. My classmates honored me by asking me to speak as their representative at the graduation ceremony. How could I begin to describe the last two weeks to the audience? How could I express to them what we had experienced? How could I tell them how much this small group of men and women with physical disabilities had challenged and pushed ourselves? I wanted them to understand that we had put everything on the line in order to develop a partnership with our new service dogs so that, with their help, we could achieve the freedom that we all so desperately wanted.

*Canine Companions for Independence puppy raiser, Jeni Exley, and Paws With A Cause service dog recipient, Marcie Davis, enjoy talking about their assistance dog experiences while puppy in training, Janice, and service dog, Morgan, lie quietly. Photograph courtesy of Franz Freibert.*

# CHAPTER FOUR

# Access to the World

Training was over and it was time to go home. I was petrified. It was easy when I knew my trainer was a few feet away, but the thought of being back in Florida all alone with Ramona was overwhelming. I felt so sad as we drove away and put more and more miles between us and the training center. But, there was no turning back now. We were graduates, she was mine, and life continued.

## OPENING NEW DOORS – STARTING A NEW AND INDEPENDENT LIFE

Ramona was by my side from that moment on, 24 hours a day, seven days a week. She was a little angel and a little stinker all in one. Luckily, we returned to Tallahassee right before Thanksgiving which gave me a few days to unpack and get into a routine before starting back to work.

I was extremely nervous about my first day at the office with Ramona. Everyone was curious about her and what she and I had experienced during training. Luckily, Ramona's puppy raiser, Michelle, worked at a bank, so Ramona was accustomed to an office environment. She quickly found a favorite spot in my office and made herself comfortable. Her big brown eyes watched as my co-workers filed in and out to gaze at her. She seemed to bask in the attention and knew she was the star.

It was extremely important that I share information about my new service dog with people in my life. I had to become comfortable explaining what a service dog was and what she did for me and how she should be treated in public. My immediate family had never experienced a dog in their home, and at first it was difficult for them to be comfortable with a dog by my side 24 hours a day, 7 days a week, holidays included. Franz has a very large family and it was difficult to explain to his small nieces and nephews why they could not play with Ramona. People had to understand that Ramona was a working dog; therefore, their contact with her was limited.

Be prepared to discuss your new service dog with many other people, who may include your landlord, employer, employees, neighbors, friends, dates, professional caretakers and their staff, and people you meet on the street. The incessant curiosity expressed by strangers in public places was one of the most challenging aspects of having a service dog for me. When you receive a service dog you must be prepared to confront the public about your dog and to explain to

*"Love me, love my dog."*
*- John Heywood*

them the proper etiquette regarding your dog. This has been one of the more difficult things for me. Some service dog recipients place a sign on their dog's backpack or harness. Talking with strangers about your service dog is definitely something you need to be prepared to address.

Over the first year, Ramona and I worked diligently to perfect our routine and to understand each other's habits, likes, and dislikes. It took time, energy, and hard work to completely trust each other. Throughout the first year, there were times when I questioned whether I had made the right decision to get a ser-

vice dog. I found out later that this is a typical experience after making such a life altering decision. I must confess that even now as Morgan approaches retirement and I am awaiting my third service dog, I continue to ask myself, "Will a service dog enable me to be more independent?" For me, the answer has always been "yes."

The beauty of our relationship was that Ramona needed me, and I needed her. I had to meet all of her needs just like she was meeting mine. I was the only one who could feed her, brush her teeth, take her to the vet, oversee her grooming, and even play with her.

Suddenly a whole new world opened up for me. I had considered myself fairly independent prior to getting Ramona. However, it soon became clear that I really was not independent, and there were numerous things I never considered until she came into my life. This same eye-opening experience is reported by many new service dog recipients. All of a sudden the impossible seems possible, and things you thought were out of your reach literally and figuratively are now obtainable. Virtually every area in your personal and professional life can be expanded and explored, including your vocation, travel opportunities, housing options, and transportation.

The increased independence afforded by a service dog can improve your quality of life and provide you with options that you thought were unavailable. Take some time and formulate a list of

*Morgan lies unobtrusively under Marcie's desk while she is at work. Courtesy of Doug Reeves.*

It can be intimidating for recipients to have to explain their service dog to curious onlookers and associates at work or school.

*Courtesy of Kim Alaburda.*

things that you have always wanted to do but felt you could not do because of your reliance on others. For example, maybe you always wanted to go to school, apply for another job, volunteer at a local charity, or take a cooking class. Whatever you dreamed of accomplishing can be realized with the assistance of a service dog. Ramona did this for me. It can happen for you, too.

After the first year with Ramona, I began to notice some changes in my own behavior. Suddenly, I grew impatient waiting for Franz to pick us up after work. I began to question myself about my independence. Franz was an absolute saint, but why shouldn't I be able to drive myself to work and go to the mall by myself to shop? One day as Ramona and I were waiting for Franz, I looked at her and said, "What do we need to really be independent?" In my

mind, the answer was a power wheelchair, an accessible van that I could drive, and a service dog. I already had the most precious one of those three things. How hard could it be to obtain the other two?

That is when my life was really transformed. Because of Ramona, I had the confidence to get an accessible van and a power wheelchair. After that, there was no stopping the two of us. For the first time in my life, I was able to run errands, go to the mall, and do anything that I wanted to do. My professional life improved. I was promoted at work and began traveling the state to fulfill my new duties. I remember Franz saying that Ramona was as much of a gift to him as she was to me. Now he did not have to worry about me as he had in the past. He knew I was in "good paws" and that, together with my service dog, I

*Marcie and Morgan travel extensively and Morgan is comfortable traversing public areas. Photo Courtesy of Doug Reeves.*

> Expect the recipient's life and outlook to change. An entire new world has opened to them.

could go anywhere and do anything. It was pure bliss and a match made in Heaven!

For me the ability to drive was equal to greater independence. In today's mobile society, transportation is one of the keys to independence. Even as an adult, I never went anywhere by myself due to my fear of becoming stranded. Ramona alleviated those fears with her ability to retrieve my dropped car keys, get the cellular telephone from my purse, and provide a sense of security that I was not alone. Franz's worst nightmare was coming true—me with a service dog, car keys, and a credit card! Yet, Franz's hope for me to become independent was becoming a reality. I could share in the daily responsibilities of our household such as going to the bank, picking up the dry cleaning, and other daily errands.

In interviewing assistance dog recipients for this book, they shared with us that getting an assistance dog helped them expand their living options. For example, getting a service dog facilitated the move from a parents', family, or group home to their own home or apartment. (Issues surrounding housing and service dog access are addressed in the next section.)

## PUBLIC ACCESS

A service dog can provide you with greater access to your community and the world. Fortunately, laws provide for and protect public access for you and your service dog. Federal laws granting access rights to service dogs include: The Rehabilitation Act of 1973, Sections 501 (federal government), 503 (federal contractors) and 504 (recipients of federal

*Morgan assists Marcie by retrieving hard to reach laundry items. Courtesy of Kim Alaburda.*

financial assistance) and the 1990 Americans with Disabilities Act (which covers most everybody). When I received my second service dog, Morgan, from Paws With A Cause, they provided me with an informational card that stated the following:

> The law in 50 states, U.S. territories, and Canadian provinces guarantees all disabled people the right to be accompanied by a specially trained dog in any public accommodation and on all public transportation. The dog user cannot be charged an extra fee because of the dog's presence and in most states the dog's user is liable for any damage the dog may cause. A dog user also has a legal right to equal accommodations in all housing. In some states the dog user may be required to produce an identification card from the school where the dog was trained. Violations of these rights may result in penal and civil damages, under state and ADA laws.

The International Association of Assistance Dog Partners (IAADP) has been a leader in advocating for public access for service dogs and their website (www.iaadp.org) provides helpful information regarding applicable laws and access issues.

Although an identification card is not required for public access in all fifty states, we recommend that you carry some type of certification or identification card that clearly identifies your dog as a trained service animal. While you cannot be denied access to public areas, there may be times when you will be questioned, and an identification card can come in handy for educating individuals and businesses.

You are not required to inform a hotel or restaurant that you are bringing an assistance dog. In some cases, hotel desk clerks and restaurant managers are more accommodating in person than they might be on the telephone. It is up to you whether or not you want to inform them in advance that you will be accompanied by an assistance dog.

*Morgan assisting Marcie with hotel registration. Courtesy of Doug Reeves.*

Recipients are not required to tell hotels, restaurants, and other public facilities that they are bringing an assistance dog.

## HOUSING ACCESS

The U.S. Department of Justice and the Department of Housing and Urban Development (HUD) are jointly responsible for enforcing the federal Fair Housing Act (42 U.S.C. §§ 3601–3619), which prohibits discrimination in housing on the basis of race, color, religion, sex, national origin, familial status, and disability. One type of disability discrimination prohibited by the Fair Housing Act is the refusal to make reasonable accommodations in rules, policies, practices, or services when such accommodations may be necessary to afford a person with a disability the equal opportunity to use and enjoy a dwelling. The Fair Housing Act requires public and private housing providers to modify policies and practices to enable people with disabilities to use and enjoy their dwellings. Dwellings under this rule can be defined as apartments, houses, nursing homes, group homes, seasonal facilities, residential facilities, mobile homes, and trailer parks; however, exemptions do exist and you should contact HUD if you have any questions. The Fair Housing Act also applies to condominiums and cooperatives, but some may fall under exception if a particular unit is owned by an individual owner who is accorded exempt status.

A "reasonable accommodation" is a change, exception, or adjustment to a rule, policy, practice, or service that may be necessary for a person with a disability to have an equal opportunity to use and enjoy a dwelling, including public and common use spaces. Since rules, policies, practices, and services may have a different effect on persons with disabilities than on other persons, treating persons with disabilities exactly the same as others will sometimes deny them an equal opportunity to use and enjoy a dwelling.

One such rule or policy a housing provider may have in place is a "no pets" policy. A tenant who is deaf may request that the provider allow him to keep a dog in his unit as a reasonable accommodation. The tenant explains that the dog is an assistance animal that will alert him to several sounds, including knocks at the door, sounding of the smoke detector, the telephone ringing, and cars coming into the driveway. The housing provider must make an exception to its "no pets" policy to accommodate this tenant. The Fair Housing Act does not define "service animal" but it does recognize that service animals are necessary for the individuals with disabilities who have them and therefore recognizes them as something other than "pets." Based on this understanding, assistance dog recipients cannot be subjected to "pet rules" such as size and weight restrictions, additional fees or access to common areas with their assistance dogs.

Housing providers may not require persons with disabilities to pay extra fees or deposits as a condition of receiving a reasonable accommodation. For example, a housing provider may not require an applicant with a hearing impairment who needs to keep an assistance animal in his unit to pay a fee or a security deposit as a condition of allowing the applicant to keep the assistance animal. However, if a tenant's assistance animal causes damage to the applicant's unit or the common areas of the dwelling, the housing provider may charge the tenant

for the cost of repairing the damage (or deduct it from the standard security deposit imposed on all tenants), if it is the provider's practice to assess tenants for any damage they cause to the premises. Failure to pay the damages could result in reports to local animal control and/or eviction although a housing provider may first be obligated to attempt resolution prior to eviction proceedings.

A provider is entitled to obtain information that is necessary to evaluate if a requested reasonable accommodation may be necessary because of an obvious or known disability. If a person's disability is obvious, or otherwise known to the provider, and if the need for the requested accommodation is also readily apparent or known, then the provider

*Joan Froling's Samoyed, Dakota, trained by Sterling Service Dogs, pulls her wheelchair down the sidewalk. Courtesy of Joan Froling.*

may not request any additional information about the requester's disability or the disability-related need for the accommodation. In order to be protected by the Fair Housing Act with regard to services animals, you should be prepared to answer the following questions to support the request for reasonable accommodation:

1) If it is not obvious, what is your disability?
2) What function does the animal serve as directly related to your disability?
3) Is the request to have the service animal reasonable?

When a person with a disability believes that he or she has been subjected to a discriminatory housing practice, including a provider's wrongful denial of a request for reasonable accommodation, she may file a complaint with HUD within one year after the alleged denial or may file a lawsuit in federal district court within two years of the alleged denial. If a complaint is filed with HUD, HUD will investigate the complaint at no cost to the person with a disability. There are several ways that a person may file a complaint with HUD:

- By placing a toll-free call to 1-800-669-9777 or TTY 1-800-927-9275;
- By completing the "on-line" complaint form available on the HUD internet site: http://www.hud.gov; or
- By mailing a completed complaint form or letter to:
  Office of Fair Housing and Equal Opportunity
  Department of Housing & Urban Development
  451 Seventh Street, S.W.,
  Room 5204
  Washington, DC 20410-2000

## TRAVEL ACCESS

Once you have a taste of the independence and freedom that a service dog will afford you, your world will quickly grow larger than just the corner grocery store or your workplace. You may find yourself with "wander lust" and begin to think about taking that trip of your dreams. The world can be your oyster with a little preparation and planning. There are many modes of travel and transportation to consider. Following are some things to consider when using different modes of transportation with a service dog.

**Car Travel** – There are a few ways to safely transport your service dog by car. Most service dogs are crate trained and may feel comfortable riding in a crate in the vehicle. Morgan did not feel comfortable riding in a crate, so I chose to place him on the back seat of my van and connect a specially purchased seat belt to his harness. Think about traveling with your service dog in a car the same way you would think about traveling with a small child. You want them to be safe and comfortable.

**Security Screenings** – With all of the heightened levels of security that we encounter today, it is imperative that you become aware of some simple tips for you and your service dog to successfully navigate a security screening process. The United States Department of Homeland Security Transportation Security Administration (www.tsa.gov) developed an informational tool for persons with disabilities and medical conditions that provides valuable information for entering security screenings at airports, passenger vessels, transit rail stations, and other forms of mass transit. These tips should apply to all forms of security screenings including state and federal buildings, court houses, and venues where large groups of people gather, such as concerts and sporting events. The Transportation Security Administration currently refers to service animals and provides the following general tips for interacting with the Transportation Security Officer(s) (TSO):

If you have a service animal, you are encouraged to inform the TSO that the animal accompanying you is a service animal and not a pet. This will provide you with an opportunity to move to the front of the screening line since the TSO may need to spend more time with you.

It is recommended that persons using an animal for assistance carry appropriate identification. Identification may include: cards or documentation, presence of a harness or markings on the harness, or other credible assurance of the passenger using the animal for their disability.

At no time during the screening process will you be required to be separated from your service animal.

TSOs have been trained not to communicate, distract, interact, play, feed, or pet service animals.

The TSO should ask permission before touching your service animal or its belongings.

You must assist with the inspection process by controlling the service animal while the TSO conducts the search. You are required to maintain control of the animal in a manner that ensures the animal cannot harm the TSO.

If you need to leave the sterile area to relieve your animal, you must under-go the full screening process again. Inform the TSO upon your return to the security checkpoint and she/he will move you to the front of the screening line to expedite the screening process. The Transportation Security Administration provides the following advice specific to service dogs:

Advise the TSO how you and your dog can best achieve screening when going through the walk-through metal detector (WTMD) as a team (i.e., whether walking together or with the service animal walking in front or behind you).

If the WTMD alarms in the situation where you and the animal have walked together, both you and the dog must undergo additional screening.

If the WTMD alarms on either you or the dog individually (because you walked through separately), additional screening must be conducted on whoever alarmed the WTMD.

If the dog alarms the WTMD, the TSO will ask the person with a disability's permission and assistance before they touch the dog and its belongings. The TSO will then perform a hand inspection of the dog and its belongings (collar, harness, leash, backpack, vest, etc.). The belongings will not be removed from the dog at any time.

**Airline Travel** – My service dogs have been frequent flyers. Currently, a service dog can travel in the cabin with you without incurring an extra fee, but there have been motions by Congress to force service dog owners to purchase a ticket for their dog. Call ahead and let the airline carrier know you have a service dog and provide any identification that will help the airline accommodate you. Realize beforehand that you may be asked to remove your

# Basic Service Dog Travel Tips

- Make sure your service dog is wearing identification tags with both your names, home address, and telephone number.
- Make sure your dog's licenses are current. You must be able to prove that your dog belongs to you so be prepared with appropriate documentation from your veterinarian.
- Be sure to keep your dog hydrated. Investigate the safety of the water supply where you are traveling and be prepared with a portable water bowl and bottled water. I have learned that Morgan does much better on any trip if he drinks bottled water.
- Be sure to bring enough food for your dog so he can maintain his diet while traveling.
- It always behooves you to call ahead to educate yourself and the transportation carrier about your service dog, whatever transportation mode you are using.
- Talk to your veterinarian about any concerns he or she may have about your dog's health and safety during your travel plans, such as parasites, diseases, illnesses, etc. Also, talk to your vet about how to deal with potential motion sickness, stomach aches, etc. I always pack some basic medications that my vet has indicated are safe for Morgan to take or use for minor illnesses, abrasions, or cuts, such as Imodium, Pepcid AC, Neosporin, etc.
- If your dog does get a stomach ache and vomits on an airplane or other mode of transportation, we have learned to carry small trash bags and gloves and have found that Club Soda or Sparkling Water will help immensely to alleviate both the stain and the smell.
- Be sure to pack a supply of all the medication(s) your dog may need while on travel.
- Find out what laws apply to your service dog at your travel destination, especially if you are traveling to an island or internationally.

*U.S. Paralympics Quad Rugby Athlete Jason Regier and his Canine Companions for Independence service dog, Newley. Photo courtesy of Kenny Hosack.*

dog's harness for security purposes, so allow extra time to clear security.

Keeping your service dog comfortable and healthy during flights requires a little preparation. Long flights, extensive security procedures, and unexpected delays can raise toileting concerns. Some of the strategies that Morgan and I have used include taking him to the bathroom right before we go through security to board the plane and taking him to the bathroom as soon as we exit the plane even before claiming my baggage. If you choose this solution, allow airline personnel to claim your baggage and retrieve them from the airline once you have given your dog a toileting opportunity. Another option would be to train your dog to relieve him or herself on a disposable pad or to request the airline's assistance in taking your dog onto the tarmac. However, not all dogs will relieve themselves on concrete.

Most people are excited to see a dog on an airplane and look forward to sitting next to you and your service dog. However for reasons such as allergies, fears, cultural issues, etc., others may object. If you find yourself in this position, talk with a flight attendant and request that either you or the other passenger be reseated. Try not to take it personally. Morgan is treated like a celebrity on most of his flights. Thanks to my service dogs I have gotten to see more of the country than I ever imagined.

**Trains and Subways** – You may encounter trains and subways as part of your daily commute or while visiting a major city. The main concern to be aware of is boarding and exiting the train or subway. Be acutely aware of obstructions, poles, gaps between the platform and train car, elevators, escalators, and hand rails and avoid getting your dog's leash entangled.

**Buses** – You may encounter a bus as part of your daily commute or while traveling. If you have to be physically transported onto the bus, you may have to request someone hold your dog while you are being transferred. It is helpful to work with your dog beforehand on how to tolerate watching you be handled by a stranger.

**Cruise Ship** – Cruises are becoming more accommodating to service dogs and travelers with disabilities. When planning your cruise, talk to the travel agent or travel planner about your specific service dog needs. The biggest question people ask us is "Where will my dog toilet on the ship?" From personal experience, most ships have a designated area (i.e., grass, sand box, etc.) available for your dog. You are still responsible for cleaning up after him or her so remember to bring lots of baggies.

## INTERNATIONAL TRAVEL

International travel is very different from traveling domestically within the contiguous United States. The best advice we can offer to you, is "Plan, plan, plan." If you are considering traveling outside of the country, keep in mind that everything regarding your service dog is country specific (i.e., vaccination requirements, public access, quarantine laws, applicable fees, etc.). We always consult each specific country's consulate website when considering traveling abroad.

The Delta Society's website has some helpful information regarding traveling abroad. They recommend learning how to say "my dog is trained to help me with my disability" in the language of the area or country you are visiting. It is also advised that you get a letter from your vet saying your dog is in good health with current vaccinations, and have the letter translated into the language of the area or the country that you are visiting. You may contact the embassy or consulate and request that they translate the vet's letter and have it signed on consulate letterhead. All of the travel tips listed above are heightened when you are traveling internationally. Long international flights and arrivals through customs can mean extensive waiting periods that can try both you and your dog's patience. Remain cognizant of all your service dog's needs during these periods and remember that your adventure awaits.

U.S. Department of Agriculture's (USDA) Animal and Plant Health Inspection Service (APHIS) has a Pet Travel Internet web page which provides basic information on domestic and international travel of common pets and other animals. Although U.S. law differentiates service animals from pets, many countries do not make such a distinction. The USDA suggests that if you have any questions or concerns for traveling with an animal to a foreign country you should contact the Veterinary Services Area Office in the state from which your dog will be exported. The USDA office also issues a document entitled *United States Interstate and International Certificate of Health Examination For Small Animals*. We recently traveled to Paris, France, and had a personal experience

## Planning for Separation

It may be difficult to think about, but in an emergency or extreme situation you might be separated from your service dog. We recommend the following tips just in case you get separated while traveling:

- Keep several pictures of your service dog in your wallet or suitcase.
- Know where the animal shelters or rescue animal organizations are located.
- Have your dog microchipped and/or tattooed for identification purposes.
- Be prepared to use alternative ways to negotiate your environment.

with obtaining this form and working with the USDA office in Albuquerque, New Mexico. If you are planning on traveling abroad, be sure and contact your local USDA Office. They can be very helpful in preparing you for what you and your service dog may encounter while traveling internationally. It does take some time to get the International Health Certificate forms completed mainly because a portion of the form has to be completed by your dog's veterinarian and the other portion must be completed by the USDA Area Veterinarian in Charge. The key is to plan ahead and to make sure you have all of the proper documentation required by the country you are visiting and the airline carrier you are using.

Assistance Dogs International has published the *Guide To Assistance Dog Laws, First Edition* which addresses international assistance dog legislation in countries having ADI member organizations. Member organizations are found in the United States, Canada, Australia, Austria, Czech Republic, England and the United Kingdom, Germany, Japan, New Zealand, Portugal, South Korea, South Africa, and Spain. This publication is designed to intro-

duce Assistance Dogs legislation so that Assistance Dogs partners and trainers have a resource guide to the rights of the working team.

When traveling to an island, including Hawaii, and to a number of foreign countries, one must be aware of additional quarantine and vaccination issues regarding rabies. Plan as far in advance as possible to allow time for necessary paperwork, vaccinations, laboratory testing, obtaining information about quarantine laws, etc. When Morgan and I traveled to Hawaii, it took eight weeks to complete the mandatory laboratory testing and paperwork. Even though of all of this preparatory work was completed on time, we were still greeted by members of the staff of the Hawaiian Department of Agriculture at the terminal gate and were whisked away to their airport laboratory for blood samples and to verify Morgan's vaccinations and paperwork. Once again, research and pre-planning is crucial to an enjoyable travel experience.

While traveling is one of my favorite hobbies, I have experienced what I would consider some dangerous situations while traveling with my service dog. For example, Franz, Ramona, and

*Courtesy of Assistance Dogs of the West.*

Only the recipient or their designee is allowed to feed or handle the service dog. If you meet an assistance dog on the street do not offer treats nor do anything to distract the dog from doing its job.

I were visiting Washington, D.C., and we were walking to the Metro subway station. As we were approaching the Metro elevator, a dog came out of a local florist shop and attacked Ramona. This dog was pure muscle, and he went straight for her throat. In the corner of my eye, I noticed Franz quickly raring back and thrusting his foot forward. He kicked the dog in the chest and the stunned dog released Ramona. This was a very close call, and Ramona was traumatized by the attack. From then on, she was uneasy around other dogs and we had to work on rebuilding her confidence. In another instance, Morgan and I were traveling across a parking lot when a strange dog approached us and became aggressive toward Morgan. I used my power wheelchair to block the dog from Morgan, and when the dog came too close, I ran over its paw. The dog retreated, and we went on our way.

As in all safety preparations, be aware of your surroundings and aware of your service dog's needs and signals. Never leave your dog alone in a car or a hotel room. Be cautious when crossing traffic and remember to always be considerate of others and pick up after your dog. With a little pre-planning and forethought, you can alleviate many travel concerns for both yourself and your service dog and have an enjoyable and memorable travel experience.

# CHAPTER FIVE

## You, Your Service Dog and Your Veterinarian

As soon as we returned to Florida from Team Training, I set up an initial introduction between Ramona and her new veterinarian. Having just learned how important Ramona's health was to her performance, I selected a veterinarian based on the advice of local puppy raisers and trainers. Even before I went to Team Training, I had looked into vet services while anticipating my new service dog. I did not realize at the time what an important step this was.

Selecting a veterinarian for your service dog is one of the most important choices you will make in his or her lifetime. Feeling comfortable and confident in your vet is critical to the success of the team. Veterinarians, much like medical doctors, have many years of formal education and extensive medical experience. Many people look to these professionals for medical advice and do not question their authority or expertise. However, no one medical professional can know *everything* there is to know about his or her patient. Even the best vet may not be familiar with the role of service dogs and may not realize that a service dog is essential to their human partner's livelihood and way of life. A vet may not fully understand the impact of a service dog's illness, retirement, and ultimate death. Whether you

have a hearing dog, a seizure dog, or any other type of assistance dog, you cannot function normally without your canine partner. Your vet must understand these realities in order to effectively serve you and your dog. As you may know, ongoing health maintenance, retirement, euthanasia, and death are important issues for you and your partner. These issues will be addressed in detail throughout the next few chapters. Here are some important things for you to keep in mind.

## CHOOSING A VETERINARIAN FOR YOUR SERVICE DOG

Let's face it, choosing a vet can be stressful whether you are a first time shopper or a seasoned animal lover. Communicating your own and your partner's special needs can be tricky and time consuming. Here are some ways to start the selection process and to initiate dialogue in a friendly and effective manner.

Word of mouth is the best predictor of good vet care. If you have the luxury of time, consult with your service dog provider agency to see if they know of any other working dog teams in your geographic area. This pursuit could not only significantly reduce your search time for a vet, but it could be the first steps toward

*"Not to hurt our humble brethren is our first duty to them, but to stop there is not enough. We have a higher mission — to be of service to them wherever they require it."*
*- St. Francis of Assisi*

## The Veterinarian's Service Dog Checklist

Welcome to the world of service dog partnerships. You, as the team's veterinarian, are embarking on a unique and rewarding journey. You will serve an essential role in the health of this service dog team. As a vet, you see and can address canine health issues which may be unknown to the human partner. You must keep in mind that you are treating a different kind of animal. This is not a family pet. You may be asked to make some difficult life changing decisions that will impact the independence and the livelihood of the human partner. Here are some suggestions that may help you along the way:

- Request and review all the paperwork related to the dog's medical history.
- Establish contact with the agency providing the service dog.
- Request a brochure and other informational material.
- Become familiar with the service dog agency's reporting requirements.
- Familiarize yourself with state and federal laws regarding assistance dogs.
- Talk with your client about each individual assistance dog's job description and physical requirements.
- You have been given the rare opportunity to share your knowledge and expertise with an amazing team. Thank you for your commitment to assistance dogs and their human partners!

building a local support network. If there are no service dogs in your area, simply consult with friends and acquaintances about their choice of veterinarians. Perhaps you already have a vet for your pets and you need to establish a special relationship with your vet for your service dog partner.

No matter how you initiate the relationship, be prepared before you make that first appointment. Prioritize your needs and your partner's needs using the following checklist. A mutual understanding and collaborative relationship will be invaluable when it comes time to make difficult decisions in the life of the service dog team.

A good veterinarian will appreciate any information and guidance to help them better serve their clients. You can facilitate this process by helping your vet find the resources they need to serve you better. Here's a simple Veterinarian's Service Dog Checklist to share with your vet.

### INDIVIDUALIZED TREATMENT PLANNING

Now that you have a vet, it is time to begin developing an understanding of the long-term issues that you and your dog will inevitably face. With healthcare, time is always of the essence; and time without your service dog means time without your independence. In times of crisis, questions abound. How quickly can you get an appointment? (The longer you have to wait for an appointment the longer you may be without your partner.) How long will the treatment take? Will my partner be incapacitated? If so, for how long? When selecting treatment options and strategies, ask yourself what's best for you and your service dog. Consider the timing and type of treatment that will provide maximum benefits to your service dog and minimum disruption to your lifestyle. Most vet care is done to accommodate the vet's schedule, but it does not always have to be that way. Talk to your vet. If your vet is not willing to negotiate treatment options, then you may need to rethink your choice of vet. What about recuperation time? It is necessary to have conversations with your vet about your dog's limitations during its recovery time. You may need to remind your vet that you need to set timelines for when your canine partner can safely return to work. If your vet understands the impact on your work, life, and safety that not having your dog creates, then he or she will be more accommodating of your needs.

A well educated and understanding vet is even more critical as your dog ages because your vet will play a central role in determining when it is time to retire your partner. Donna, a social activist with brittle bone disease, was partnered with Derrick, a chocolate Labrador Retriever. The two had worked together for over a decade when Donna started noticing signs of Derrick's aging. Donna hesitated to share this insight with Derrick's provider agency, but she knew in her heart she could not ignore it for long and it had to be addressed. Donna spoke openly with her vet about her observations and concerns about Derrick. Donna stated, "I had to really start thinking about Derrick's needs instead of mine." Her vet provided a list of the commands Derrick could no longer perform safely. Fortunately for Donna, her physical condition had improved and she no longer needed him to do some of the more strenuous tasks that concerned her vet, such as pulling her wheelchair. Honesty and a good working relationship with her vet allowed Donna to ex-

tend Derrick's working life while at the same time enabling her agency time to prepare for a successor dog. Losing your service dog may not easily fit into the predetermined phases of retirement and euthanasia. However difficult it may be to talk about these issues, planning for and managing an individualized health plan may help ease the burden of decision making in times of crisis.

*Courtesy of Assistance Dogs of the West.*

**Health care is an important, and costly, consideration for recipients. Choose a qualified vet who is responsive to you and your service dog's needs.**

*Dogs with helpful hearts deserve the best of care. Courtesy of Assistance Dogs of the West.*

# CHAPTER SIX

## Keeping Your Service Dog Healthy and Happy

After receiving Ramona, Franz and I were showered with gifts similar to the way a new mom and dad are showered with gifts when they bring their baby home. As part of my education and training, Canine Companions for Independence provided us with a basic starter kit that included samples of the food Ramona was currently eating, a toothbrush, stainless steel bowls, a new backpack, a leash, and various other items. The puppy raisers in my community tried to give me items that would help in the bonding process and to remind us that this relationship was not all about work—it was also about play.

Most service dog agencies include information and education regarding the diet and nutrition, grooming, and exercise needs of a service dog. One of the things CCI stressed was that service dogs are not robots. They must be fed, watered, toileted, groomed, receive regular exercise, ongoing medical evaluation, and lots of love. Up to that time, the dogs in my life had all lived outdoors and were very different from the trained service dog that would be by my side twenty-four hours a day. I quickly learned that my responsibility to Ramona was equal to her responsibility to me. It became apparent that we needed

to develop a daily routine that included all her needs.

### NUTRITION AND WEIGHT CONTROL

Nutrition and weight control are vital to your dog's well-being. Proper nutrition and weight maintenance can directly impact her physical health, behavior, temperament, sleep, and emotional stability. Your dog's diet and weight will ultimately affect her ability to perform as a service dog. This is why it is so important that you are aware of what and how much food your dog is eating. Whether you feed dry food, canned food, a raw diet, or a combination, the key to good nutrition and weight control is understanding your dog's ideal weight and how diet affects his or her overall health and work performance. Many people have questions about raw or natural diets. We suggest consulting your veterinarian (or a veterinarian that specializes in raw diets).

When you receive your service dog, the provider agency should talk with you about the type of diet your dog has been receiving and provide guidance regarding your dog's ideal weight. I have learned a great deal about canine nutrition over the past twelve years. Morgan's

*Each friend represents a world in us, a world possibly not born until they arrive, and it is only by this meeting that a new world is born.*
*– Anaïs Nin, the Diary of Anaïs Nin, Volume II*

in obtaining the medication to protect against heartworm. My service dogs have always been on a heartworm regime. They get a chewable tablet once a month to prevent heartworm disease.

Vitamin supplements, minerals, and nutritional oils may enhance the health and coat of your dog. Talk with your vet during different stages of your service dog's life to see what, if any, supplements he or she may recommend. For example, because of the dry climate in the Southwest, Morgan struggles with dry skin. His vet recommended that I add fish oil to his food and it has made a tremendous difference in the appearance and feel of his coat as well as reducing itchy skin.

## GROOMING

Good grooming is connected to good health. Grooming is important because poor skin, nail, dental, and ear conditions can lead to health problems and cause distractions that impact your dog's ability to perform its job. Regular grooming is recommended for all service dogs. What constitutes regular grooming depends on the specific breed of your dog. Just because a dog has a short hair coat does not mean he does not need to be groomed.

The first decision you need to make is whether you will personally groom your dog or whether you will select a professional groomer. Patricia (Trish) Finn, a certified International Society of Canine Cosmetologists (ISCC) Master Groomer, highly recommends professional grooming for service dogs regardless of the breed. She understands the importance of quality grooming which may be difficult for an inexperienced individual to perform.

Preferably, professional groomers should be trained and certified by the ISCC because of the strenuous training and certification standards. Regardless of the groomer you select, never assume that they will understand the role of a service dog or have all the pertinent information for grooming your particular breed. Trish encourages service dog owners to research information regarding appropriate grooming for their dog breed prior to their first grooming appointment. Also, talk with your service dog agency about grooming or refer to the American Kennel Club (AKC) website for information regarding breed clubs in your area. These breed clubs can provide you with the best information on grooming for your specific dog breed.

If you groom your dog at home either by choice or for financial reasons, here are a few suggestions. First, seek assistance from a local breeder of your service dog's specific breed who participates

## Safety Tips

**Tip 1:** An important safety tip is to be sure your groomer dries your dog by hand and never uses a cage dryer, as these have been associated with heat stroke and death.

**Tip 2:** Service dogs depend on their feet. Be patient and gentle when engaging in nail trimming. Caution your groomer or veterinarian to be aware of any foot related concerns.

**Tip 3:** Check your dog's ears for any potential issues such as ear mites and other parasites, hair growth, etc., that may prevent proper air circulation and create pain and yeast infections.

**Tip 4:** Use a knuckle bone to help your dog naturally have good oral hygiene and to remove tartar.

in dog shows. These individuals tend to genuinely love dogs and have extensive experience caring for them and may be willing to help others do the same. Local breeders can be identified by contacting the AKC. Important elements of good grooming include not only skin and coat care but ongoing nail, ear, and dental care.

Clip and file your dog's nails every one to three weeks to keep them short. This prevents the dogs' nails from scratching floors, tearing or getting caught in something, improves their footing, and keeps snow and ice from building up. Working dogs depend heavily on their feet and as a result can be extremely sensitive to any type of activity involving their feet, including nail trimming. If you or a family member are unable to handle the nail clipping, you will need to have a groomer, veterinarian, breeder or friend attend to it on a regular basis. Ramona and Morgan struggled with every nail trimming session, so I always cautioned groomers and veterinarians that their feet were sensitive.

Check your dogs ears on a weekly basis for signs of foul odor, wax buildup, itching or infection. Ask your veterinarian to show you how to clean the ears properly and to recommend an ear cleaning product that is right for your dog. Watch your service dog's eyes for signs of redness, excessive tearing, or matter. Keep a good eye wash on hand, or use boric acid or artificial tears made for contact lens wearers to rinse the eyes if there is mild irritation. More severe irritation requires an immediate trip to the veterinary clinic. For more information talk to your veterinarian or a professional groomer.

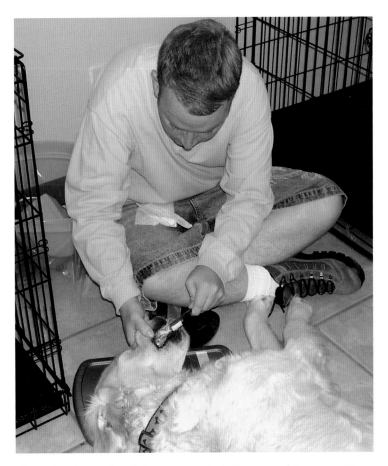

*Daily brushing of teeth is recommended. Courtesy of Assistance Dogs of the West.*

Regular dental care is both a hygiene and a health care consideration for your service dog. Regular brushing is often recommended. You can buy toothpaste for dogs and toothbrushes over the Internet or at specialty stores. However, some veterinarians and groomers believe that this is an additional chemical exposure that may be unnecessary. Trish, Morgan's groomer, suggested thinking about how your dog would naturally take care of himself. She recommended periodically providing your dog with a knuckle bone to help remove tartar. She stressed giving your dog bones that will not splinter (i.e., no chicken bones) and cause safety concerns. When giving bones, you should also be aware of any protein allergies. For example, Morgan is violently allergic to beef, so I only give him ham bones. There are numerous commercial products to help keep your dog's teeth and breath clean: tartar control treats, chew toys and ropes, special food, etc. If your dog will tolerate it, you can remove the tartar yourself using a scaling tool. Otherwise, dental care should be managed by your veterinarian. In some states professional groomers will do this, but in other states they are prohibited from providing any type of dental cleaning.

If the tartar buildup is so heavy that routine cleaning does not remove it, or if your dog has red or infected gums, professional teeth cleaning under anesthesia is necessary. Older dogs may require this at least once a year. Others, especially the large breeds, may be sensitive to anesthesia so that your vet may recommend it less frequently. Ne-

glecting broken or infected teeth or gums can lead to serious health problems, such as heart disease, that will shorten your dog's life.

## EQUIPMENT

Your service dog may be provided with items such as brushes, clippers, backpacks, and other equipment necessary for good health and grooming. If not, there are many commercial suppliers that you can purchase these items from either online or at specialty stores (see References).

Other supplies that you will want to have readily available are items to assist you in cleaning up after your dog. I keep small sandwich bags and paper towels in Morgan's zippered backpack to enable me to quickly clean up after him both at home and while on travel. We use a

## Service Dog Emergency Kit

Create a Service Dog Emergency Kit that contains the following supplies (you may want to group these items in a pack that your dog can carry). Emergency Kit items may include:

- Supply of any medications your animal is taking
- A weeks supply of food and water
- Portable bowl
- Blanket
- Favorite toy
- Extra leash, collar and harness
- Copy of all current vaccinations and health records, license numbers, microchip numbers, and tags
- Medication and feeding schedule
- Manual can opener and spoon
- Plastic bags and paper towels for pick up
- Several pictures of your animal
- First Aid Kit

## Service Dog First Aid Kit

Essential to your emergency kit is your Service Dog First Aid Kit. This kit should include the following:

- Kaopectate for diarrhea
- Human rectal suppositories for constipation
- Peptobismol for an upset stomach
- Coated low-dose aspirin for pain
- Neosporin or triple antibiotic for wounds
- Styptic pencil or powder to stop bleeding nails
- Scissors
- Bandages and gauze pads
- Calendula gel
- Hydrocortisone spray for itching
- Nail trimmer
- Rubber gloves
- Stethoscope
- Digital thermometer
- Saline solution for cleaning wounds
- Tweezers for removing thorns or splinters
- Different sizes of bandaging tape
- Ace bandage
- First Aid Book
- A nylon stocking or gauze to use for a muzzle if needed
- A stretchy round plastic tube for a tourniquet
- Something to measure medication: a syringe without the needle, measuring spoons or a liquid measuring tube sold at drugstores
- An ice pack for swelling

pooper scooper purchased from a pet supply store to clean up our backyard on a regular basis.

In addition to these everyday essentials, we highly recommend assembling a service dog First Aid Kit and an emergency kit for home and vehicle for both minor injuries and potentially major catastrophes at home or while traveling. Talk to your vet about any specific items that should be included for your dog. We have learned firsthand that a little planning can go a long way in an emergency situation.

## HEALTHY PAWS

It is important to realize that working dogs are often sensitive to the condition of their paws. Their livelihood and your independence depend upon them. In order to maintain the health of your partner's paws consider the following environmental conditions:

- If you live, work, or travel to a high temperature climate, be aware that the pavement your dog is walking on can be extremely hot. Watch for signs such as your partner continually lifting his

*Morgan relaxing after a hard day of work. Courtesy of Kim Alaburda.*

Service dogs are not robots. They require love, care, and play!

or her feet. Keep a water bottle handy and use the water to cool your dog's paws should they become overheated. Immediately get your dog to a cooler surface area. If it is that warm, then perhaps it is time for both of you to take a break and get a drink of water.

- If you live, work, or travel to a cold temperature climate with ice and snow, be aware of salt sticking in the hair between your dog's toes. This can lead to dryness, cracking, and even bleeding. Keep your dog's paws clean and free of all debris.
- If you are traveling over rough terrain (rocks, gravel, thorny vegetation, etc.), watch for signs of bloody or bruised paws.

You may want to purchase booties for your dog's paws, but keep in mind some canines will not tolerate such items. When I am traveling, I try to keep a water bottle available so I can pour water over Morgan's paws to reduce heat, clean away salt, remove gravel, etc.

## EXERCISE AND PLAY

The most impressive thing about service dogs is that they can practically talk to their human partner and will clearly communicate to you when they are ready to play. My current service dog, Morgan, will open drawers and pull out toys at his regular play time even if I am immersed in another activity. We encourage you to develop a routine around exercise and play time and to make it a priority. Similar to set feeding times, having a set exercise and play time can help you identify any potential health problems that your service dog may be experiencing. For example, if your toy motivated dog is suddenly uninterested in play, you have a clear indicator that something is wrong, and you need to investigate further.

Exercise and play is a stress reliever for most dogs and is required for mental balance. Shedding their harness or backpack is akin to kicking off those high heel shoes or taking off that stuffy tie. It signals that work is over and it is time to relax and play. Most service dog agencies recommend that service dogs have their backpacks or harnesses removed before engaging in play activities. My fenced in yard provides a safe outdoor place for Morgan to play. When we are traveling, Morgan can become stressed and needs an opportunity to relieve his anxiety through play. We try to find a safe location such as a fenced in area or playground where he can play fetch or have some freedom of movement. If not, he is accustomed to playing fetch in a hotel room. There are many opportunities for play time activities, and your dog will communicate to you what activity he or she prefers. Such play time activities may include going for a stroll outside, playing fetch, going swimming, playing Frisbee, an outing at a dog park for a free run with other animals, a visit to the local pet store, etc. Whatever the activity, the most important thing is take time to play safely and have fun with your service dog.

*Janice IV, Canine Companion for Independence service dog in training, getting a treat from her puppy raiser Jeni Exley during a break from work at Craig Hospital. Photo courtesy of Franz Freibert.*

*Dakota, trained by Sterling Service Dogs, carries groceries to the house. Courtesy of Joan Froling.*

# CHAPTER SEVEN
## Illness and Retirement

Sometimes life changes come at the most unexpected times. When Franz graduated from Florida State University in September 1996 and accepted a job as a physicist at Los Alamos National Laboratory in New Mexico, we packed up all our belongings and headed west. Ramona quickly adapted to the new climate and our new life in Santa Fe, and fortunately I landed a job shortly after our arrival.

Still, it was not an easy transition. It was very difficult for me to leave my work in Florida. We didn't know a soul in New Mexico and we had hit several barriers when we first arrived: difficulty in finding accessible housing, mechanical problems with my van, and other obstacles that life sometimes throws our way. Ramona was by my side through it all. She went to job interviews with me, enabled me to run all the errands entailed with moving into a new home, and comforted me when I was homesick for Tallahassee.

In December 1996, shortly after moving to Santa Fe, Ramona and I began our new job together. Soon we began to fall in love with the people and landscape of Santa Fe. We created our new home and became active in the community. She enjoyed the snow in

the winter and the low humidity and moderate temperatures in the summer. Life was blissful again until October 1998.

Franz and I had just returned from visiting our family in Mississippi. We were fast asleep when I was awoken out of a deep sleep by a loud crash in the living room. Something was wrong. It sounded as if someone had broken down our front door. Franz leaped out of bed and I jumped into my wheelchair and zoomed into the living room. Ramona was standing by the front door. There were drops of blood on the carpet. Her nose was bloodied and it appeared she ran smack into the front door. She immediately ran to me with a dazed look on her face. Franz and I embraced her and each other. It had scared us to death. What was wrong? Why had she bolted out of bed like that? Ramona had never behaved like that before. She looked all right, just confused. She looked at me as if she wanted to apologize for getting me out of bed, but seemed relieved that I came to her. We all got back into bed, but Franz and I were very distressed about her and wondered what in the world had just happened.

The next morning I called the vet and took her in to be examined. The vet

*"A dog is the only thing on earth that loves you more than he loves himself."*
*- Josh Billings*

*Morgan retrieving hard to reach items in public. Photo Courtesy of Doug Reeves.*

conducted a full set of spinal x-rays and found multiple bone spurs. He felt Ramona had pinched a nerve the night before which had caused her excruciating pain and caused her to bolt. He prescribed Rimadyl and Cosequin and calmly told me her working life was over. I was in shock. How could this be? Ramona was only seven years old. I thought her working life was 10-12 years. He could not be right. I immediately called the CCI office in California. They told me to send them her x-rays. After a few days, I spoke with the CCI office and they confirmed the vet's assessment. They recommended she be retired and immediately began talking to me about the upcoming training class for her replacement. My head was spinning. I began to panic as I asked myself, "How can I go to work by myself? How can I go out at night to meetings? What am I going to do?" I quickly got my calendar and began canceling appointments and meetings. All

the fear of being a woman with a disability came rushing back. My independence and confidence began to fade, and the fears of being out in the world alone came creeping back into my mind. CCI told me to take a few days and think things over. They asked if there was a family member with whom Ramona might live. I thought to myself, "What? Give her away?" That was out of the question. We had no family in New Mexico plus Ramona was going to need expensive medicine and constant medical oversight. I could not give those responsibilities to someone else. She had given her life for me, and now it was time for me to focus completely on her.

Later, CCI contacted and notified me that I was accepted into their February 1998 class. I agreed, knowing in my heart that I had no intention of attending that class. I was not ready to replace my angel. How could I betray her by bringing another dog into our home so quickly?

To make matters worse, Ramona did not understand why she could not go everywhere with me anymore. This dog had been my shadow for five years and now I was leaving to go to work without her. She would stand at the door and bark. In my mind, I could hear her asking me, "Why can't I go? Did I do something wrong? Are you angry with me?" My heart broke every time I left our home. So, I started limiting my departures and my time away from home. I started feeling like I could not go anywhere without her. I was loosing my independence all over again.

## WITNESSING THE SIGNS OF AGING

Most of us look forward to the day when we can retire from the daily 8:00 A.M.

*Mindy, retired Paws with a Cause service dog. Courtesy of Alicia Chatman.*

to 5:00 P.M. grind, purchase that Winnebago and drive across the country to see the world's largest ball of twine. Few service dog recipients, however, look forward to the day when their working dog must hang up her harness. Anyone who has a working dog dreads the day when those little signs of aging can no longer be ignored. Any indication of illness or aging can be stressful for someone who relies on the physical abilities of a service dog. The fears and questions in the back of every recipient's mind can be overwhelming. When their partner becomes too ill to work or experiences an illness that may ultimately result in retirement, the human team member must face some agonizing decisions. With a little guidance, forethought and planning, this can be a natural transition similar to our own retirement.

As we shared with you earlier, Donna and Derrick were together for eleven glorious years when Donna began to notice that Derrick, her

**The time when a service dog can no longer work can be emotionally traumatic for the recipient.**

chocolate Labrador Retriever, was starting to slow down. Donna found herself in her vet's office because she knew deep in her heart she could no longer avoid Derrick's inevitable retirement. Fortunately, Donna's vet was comforting and supportive and together they developed a plan to slowly move Derrick from a full time service dog to retirement. Also, Donna's physical condition had improved, so she needed Derrick to perform less physically demanding activities. This provided her the necessary time to prepare emotionally for his retirement and to begin thinking about the possibility of a successor dog. This respite also enabled her provider agency to identify a successor dog. Donna's willingness to fully in-

## Important Questions About Your Service Dog's Retirement

- Is your dog's retirement process going to be gradual or immediate?
- Can your dog stay in the home or is there a need to explore alternative placement such as returning the dog to the agency, the original puppy raiser, a family member, etc.?
- How will your dog's retirement affect your current lifestyle? How are you going to deal with not having a service dog for a period of time?
- How does this impact your financial situation?
- Is it time to consider a successor dog and what does that mean?
- Many of these decisions are not solely dependent on you and may require the expertise of your provider agency, veterinarian, family and friends.

volve her provider agency and her veterinarian afforded her a support team. They worked together to make all the difficult decisions regarding Derrick's retirement. Donna loved Derrick dearly, and even though it terrified her to think of how his retirement would impact her independence, she bravely put Derrick's needs and well-being first. Whether your service dog is young or maturing, every sign of illness or age sets off an internal alarm in the back of your mind forcing you to acknowledge your dependence on each other.

## TALKING TO YOUR VET ABOUT RETIREMENT

Having a good relationship with your vet is paramount when you are making the major decision of retirement. Like Donna, taking the first step and talking to your vet openly and honestly about your service dog's deteriorat-

ing health may be gut-wrenching. It is not unheard of or out of the question to seek a second opinion; however, be aware that the stress of losing your service dog may cloud your ability to accept your vet's recommendations. When I found out that Ramona had to be retired, I wanted to resist it at all costs. I could not believe that my vet was making this life changing decision for Ramona and me without batting an eye. My provider agency provided a second opinion. Ramona endured an intensive series of x-rays that were then express-delivered to the provider agency. After an agonizing period of waiting, my worst fears were confirmed and Ramona was immediately retired. I had put her and my wallet through some unnecessary strenuous activities, but I wanted to be sure that her working life was really over.

With any loss, shock and disbelief are very likely to be your first responses.

Be gentle with yourself; give yourself some time to let the news sink in before making any drastic changes or decisions. Whether your service dog's retirement is gradual like Derrick's or immediate like Ramona's, the major issues are the same with a different level of urgency.

## WHAT NOW?

Once you have come to the realization that your service dog is going to be retired, you have to ask yourself if your service dog can stay in your home or if there is a need to explore alternative placements. What happens to your service dog upon retirement may depend on your provider agency's policies and any contracts or agreements that you signed when you received your dog. In the excitement of receiving your dog, you may not remember even discussing or acknowledging the retirement process. Call your provider agency to discuss your options and responsibilities. Every agency is different, but some of the possible scenarios include: returning the dog to the provider agency, placing the dog in another home, or simply keeping them at home on non-working status. These scenarios only scratch the surface of the possibilities. Please keep in mind that each individual dog and agency is different. When I shared with Franz that my provider agency encouraged me to find another home for Ramona, his response was, "Are you kidding me? Let's dye her blonde and move to Canada!"

Ramona was an integral part of our family and the thought of sending her to live with someone else was unimaginable. How could I leave her in the care of someone else when she had devoted

## Strategies For An Impending Retirement

- Prepare a list of the tasks that your service dog has to perform in order for you to function adequately.
- Realistically discuss with your vet the tasks that your service dog can safely perform without further jeopardizing his or her health.
- Explore the medical costs for maintaining your service dog's working status, i.e., medications, treatments, office visits, etc.
- Discuss a time frame for your service dog's partial or full retirement with your dog's provider agency, family, and friends.

her life to me? I felt it was my turn to take care of her and, fortunately, I had the monetary resources and family support to do so. I was lucky, but not everyone has this luxury. Some other things to think about include:

- How will your dog's retirement affect your current lifestyle? How are you going to deal with not having a working dog for a period of time?
- How does this impact your financial situation? Vacation, time off from work, vet bills, medication, assistance from another person, double expenses of maintaining two dogs, etc.
- Is it time to consider a successor dog and what does that mean: timeframe, expenses, adjustment, introduction of the new service dog into your home?

Retirement for your service dog means change for both you and your dog. For your dog it means less work, and for you it could mean more work. It will take work to learn how to live

*Jeff Fazio and Knight. Courtesy of Alicia Chatman.*

without your service dog, and it takes work to learn to live with a successor dog. The reality is, in many ways, your service dog is a loyal employee who has been with you through thick and thin, who knows your strengths and weaknesses, and has figured out how to traverse them given all the variables. This is why many people with service dogs resist their dog's retirement as I did with Ramona, but we do it because we want to honor them and their service to us.

## PLANNING FOR EUTHANASIA

Euthanasia is a dreaded topic and is often avoided until it is inevitable. However, we feel it is imperative to include a brief discussion and plan for euthanasia in the development of a relationship with your vet and your dog. The following contrasting stories shed some light on the importance of planning for euthanasia.

Jeff graciously shared the story of his last months with his loyal service dog, Spinner. As Spinner approached her twelfth birthday, she suddenly collapsed and was diagnosed with an inoperable tumor on her heart known as "cardiac sarcoma." The vet warned him that Spinner's time was limited. Jeff responded by relaxing the rules and allowing Spinner to "have a ball." He indulged her desires for treats, etc. As her condition worsened, Jeff made the

Each agency has its own rules about what happens to the retired service dog. Talk to your agency about their policies regarding retirement during the application process long before you will need the information.

dreaded final telephone call to the vet. Looking into Spinner's eyes, knowing that he was powerless to help the dog who had been so helpful to him for so many years, was the most horrible part of Jeff's experience. Gratefully, Jeff had a compassionate and flexible vet who came to his home to euthanize Spinner in familiar surroundings. Spinner's vet gave Jeff plenty of time to say good-bye before performing the procedure under Spinner's favorite tree.

Although euthanasia is often referred to as "putting an animal to sleep," those of us who have actually witnessed this procedure know that it is not that subtle and sometimes not at all peaceful. Sherry, a woman with hearing loss, described her painful experience with the loss of her hearing dog, Shep. Shep suffered from lymphoma which did not respond to chemotherapy. Sherry realized that euthanasia was inevitable. She called a friend who had agreed in advance to accompany her and together they took Shep to the vet. Because Shep was so tense, Sherry requested a shot of valium to help him relax. While waiting for the shot to take affect, Shep sat up inquisitively as he noticed that Sherry had stuck her hand in her pocket where she always kept treats. Sherry was shaken and felt like an executioner. She "…was putting him to death and he was begging for treats." They forgot to ask the vet how much time they would have together before he returned, and this uncertainty increased their anxiety. When the vet returned, Sherry requested to stay in the room. She was overwhelmed when the medication was administered and she had to turn away. When she turned back around he was

## The Euthanasia Plan

The following is a list of suggested items to discuss with your vet when developing your written euthanasia plan. We also suggest you and your vet sign and date the plan together.

**WHAT IS EUTHANASIA?** Have your vet explain to you the details of the euthanasia procedure, including what drugs are used and for what purposes. For example, will your dog receive a muscle relaxant or anti-anxiety drug, and how long before it takes affect? Discuss time elements from beginning to end.

**WHAT IS YOUR CRITERIA FOR EUTHANASIA?** What are the signs when euthanasia is imminent? Know ahead of time how your vet will evaluate when it is most humane and when there are no other alternatives.

**LOCATION?** Talk to your vet about all of your options. What location would best meet you and your partner's needs? Is your vet willing to make a house call?

**SAYING GOOD-BYE:** Once the euthanasia decision has been made, establish with your vet how much time you will have alone with your partner to say good-bye.

**SUPPORT:** Identify a friend or loved one who is willing to accompany you and include their contact information. Always have a back up person.

**POST PROCEDURE:** How much time will you have with your partner after she or he has been euthanized?

**ARRANGEMENTS:** What type of arrangements would you like to make and who is responsible for each element? For example: cremation, urn selection, burial, transportation, pick-up of cremains, etc. Discuss costs and methods of payment.

**ADDITIONAL THOUGHTS AND WISHES:** Anything else that might make this transition easier for you and your partner.

lying in her friend's lap. The vet staff then carried Shep to her car so he could be taken for cremation.

Sherry's forethought to take a friend allowed her to manage a difficult situation. Although thinking about the loss of your partner in advance may be painful and uncomfortable, planning will empower you at a critical time in your partnership. We highly recommend you create a euthanasia plan with your vet at a time when you are calm and not in crisis. Keep a copy handy for yourself and request that your vet place a copy of the plan in your partner's file to be accessed when needed.

## CHAPTER EIGHT
# The Death of a Service Dog

The new millennium was upon us, and I considered myself the luckiest woman in town to have two dedicated service dogs living with me. Little did I know that my time with Ramona was quickly dwindling. When we returned from a winter holiday trip, Ramona seemed happier than ever to see us. I remember her jumping on me when I came in the door and thinking how much that must have hurt her back, but how wonderful it was to be able to embrace her. Franz and I counted our blessings as the year came to an end and the new millennium was beginning. I commented to him that Morgan and I had been together almost a year and I felt that we were finally a strong working team.

On January 16, 2000, we awoke and prepared for work as any normal day. Franz let Ramona and Morgan out into the backyard before breakfast. As I prepared their food, he let them back into the house. Morgan ran to his bowl while Ramona hesitated. This was not her typical behavior. Ramona loved two things—breakfast and dinner.

She slowly ate her breakfast and then regurgitated it on the kitchen floor. We thought maybe she had eaten some grass outside or perhaps she had a stomach ache. Ramona lay down on the kitchen floor and looked at me with those big brown eyes. Something was wrong. I was planning to work at home that day, so Franz said he would take her to the vet on his way to work. She appeared so weak, Franz carried her to his car and off to the vet. The vet called me around 9:00 A.M. and said she felt Ramona had severe back pain and we needed to increase her medicine. Other than that, she appeared fine and Franz could pick her up on his way home.

I got a telephone call from the vet around 2:30 P.M. She said, "Marcie, something is wrong with Ramona." She went on to tell me that Ramona had collapsed in her kennel when someone offered her a treat and that she had called a specialist to come to her office and administer an ultrasound to get more information than the x-rays revealed. I said, "I'm on my way." I did not know how I was going to get dressed and get to that vet's office, but I did not care. Somehow I would manage. I threw on the easiest thing I could find and dashed out the door. When I arrived, they whisked me into an examination room. My vet came in and I could see she was shaken. She leaned over the examination table and told me Ramona had a tumor on her heart known as visceral-hemangiosarcoma and it had started hemorrhaging. There was nothing she

*"I carry Spinner with me all the time. It sort of blended in with who you are. She made a profound effect on my life beyond her commands. It opened my world up tremendously. It's like riding on the coat tails of a celebrity."*
*- Jeff Fazio*

could do. My angel was slipping through my hands, and I was helpless to stop it.

I could not stand being in that little examination room. I apologized as I ran out the door. I called Franz on my cell phone and screamed to him that Ramona was dying. He left work right away, and time seemed to drag on for years before he arrived. They never came out and said it, but they would not let me see Ramona without Franz present. When he came, we immediately went to the back of the vet's office. As we turned the corner, I could see Ramona lying on an examination table with her back to us. Her tail began to wag as she heard my wheelchair approaching. I was so thankful that she knew I was there. The way the room was arranged and the way she was lying on the table, I could not reach her. I asked them to turn her around so I could touch her head. They graciously responded to my request. When they turned her, I could roll my wheelchair up to the table and I held her head and began kissing and talking to her. Her tail was wagging, and she seemed so happy to see us as we began lavishing all the love in our hearts on her. She looked so sick and weak. Franz and I were crying uncontrollably as we caressed her. She was so cold. Her feet and ears were cold. She was shivering and shaking, but she was still wagging her tail. The vet told us that one of the chambers of her heart was bleeding into the pericardial sac (the sac in which the heart is contained). Her heart was basically trying to pump blood against its own pressure. Her heart beat was getting weaker and weaker. All this jargon meant that she was dying and there was nothing we could do. After talking with the vet and evaluating her prognosis, the only thing we could do was ease her suffering with euthanasia.

We held her, kissed her, and whispered to her for an hour before the inevitable. The vet prepared the shot and, as we held Ramona, she injected it into her intravenous drip. Ramona raised her head as if she was alert and looked at her body and then her head collapsed on the table and her tongue fell through her lips. Her eyes were open and her fur felt like velvet. She was gone.

I didn't want to leave her there, but now what? It was over. My angel had flown away. My heart was broken and my entire body ached. Franz and I left the vet's office in our separate vehicles. It was dusk and until then I had never noticed how somber and sacred dusk could be.

As I pulled into the driveway, I realized that in my haste to get to Ramona, I left Morgan at home. He was my service dog, we were rarely apart. As I entered our house, Morgan pounced on me. He was so happy to see me. He had his toy in his mouth and was begging me to throw it. "Wait a minute," I thought. "I can't play with you when my angel's soul has barely left this earth." I felt extremely guilty for having such a young, vivacious animal at my feet. How could I possibly play with him now? Franz got Morgan's attention and tried to subdue him, but it was impossible. He was ecstatic that we were home and it was his dinner time and play time.

## SUDDEN LOSS OF LIFE – MAKING GOOD DECISIONS IN A BAD SITUATION

Even if you provide the best possible care for your canine partner, there is always the looming possibility of sudden loss. If you are a member of a service dog team, the possibility of catastrophic illness is always present. Regardless of the cause, the sudden death of a canine partner is a unique and shocking experience. If this has happened to you, you are not alone.

Kevin described his Golden Retriever service dog, Spanky, as a ham with a goofy smile. Spanky was the best man at Kevin's wedding. Kevin relied on him to be his arms and legs 24 hours a day, 7 days a week.

Shortly after returning from his honeymoon, Kevin noticed that Spanky was not holding food down and his abdomen was swollen. Kevin, trying not to panic, called his provider agency to get their help in finding a specialist. The specialist was located in another city, further complicating things for Kevin. At this critical time, when all he wanted to do was support Spanky, Kevin had to let him go away for treatment. Not only was Kevin facing the possibility of losing his dog, but for the first time in years he was without the partner who provided constant service and safety. Luckily, Kevin's sister was able to visit with Spanky while he was away for treatment, which made Kevin feel more at ease.

During a conference call with the specialist, Kevin was informed that Spanky had an enlarged spleen and needed surgery. He was told to prepare himself for the worst. Surgery revealed that Spanky had advanced liver cancer and few options – chemotherapy, to put him down later, or to put him down while he was still under anesthesia. In this crisis situation, Kevin selflessly put his own wants and needs aside and tried to focus on what was best for Spanky. He came to the heart wrenching conclusion that it was probably best for Spanky if he was put down while he was still under the anesthesia.

No one wants to prepare for the worst when they are enjoying a vibrant relationship with their working dog. One recipient we interviewed remarked, "Losing your [working] dog is something that has to be discussed prior to that day." Never is it more evident that service dogs are not pets, but partners, than when we are faced with their retirement and death.

The sudden loss of life of your canine partner may result in your inability to perform normal daily functions. When you are asked to make good decisions in bad situations, remember to keep things simple and focus on the following three basic strategies:

- Allow yourself time to be in crisis mode.
- Identify your support system.
- Take care of only those immediate things that you can not put off.

Allow yourself time to be in crisis. Most people have physical symptoms in reaction to emotions that can be exaggerated when in crisis. Nausea, headache, backache, shortness of breath, difficulty swallowing, sore throat, hyperactivity, and lethargy are among the many common

**Never is it more evident that service dogs are not pets, but partners, than when we are faced with their retirement and death.**

physical reactions. And of course, cognitive reactions such as feeling like you can't think clearly, having difficulty remembering, and having poor concentration are to be expected. Every one will have their own unique reaction. You honestly cannot plan for how you are going to react in a crisis. You will not fully know how you will react until you are there, but if you are not willing to accept help, it will probably be worse. It is okay to withdraw at the beginning, but be careful not to alienate the people you may need to call upon in the near future. Kevin's initial reaction to Spanky's death was to retreat into his own private world, "I just told everyone to leave me alone. I knew I didn't want to be bothered. I just tried to keep busy." For the first couple of days, they complied and left him alone. But once he came out a little bit, his parents and wife were very supportive. He reflects on that period, "No one really knew what this dog meant to me until I lost him."

*Identify your support system* because at this difficult time the more support you have the more likely your emotional, physical, and financial needs will be met. Even simple tasks may be very difficult. Before any crisis occurs, take a moment and formulate your own personal safety network. Make a list of those people you trust and who can support you in a time of need. When you are compiling this list consider not only those closest to you, but also those close to your dog, which may include his or her veterinarian, provider agency, and puppy raiser. The purpose of identifying your safety network is to ensure that you do not have to carry the burden of this incredible loss alone. Even the act of informing people about the death can be dreadful. Your support network can help you with this and other activities of daily living that may seem too difficult to accomplish at this time. It may even take some time for you to discern what you actually need from them. However, by mobilizing them, you are putting them on notice that you may be calling on them for assistance. They might be feeling helpless and your efforts to contact them will give them something productive to do. Enlist your support network to assist you with cooking, shopping, getting your medications, covering you at work, and to listen to your story.

*Take care of only those immediate things that you can not put off* because when in crisis mode, there are some decisions that you do not have a second chance to make. Even though Ramona's death was sudden, her body remained at my vet's office for three days before cremation, allowing me time to gather my thoughts and emotions. The next morning, it occurred to me that I needed to have some of her shiny, velvet black hair as a keepsake. A few years earlier, a friend gave me a Native American medicine bag. Inside the bag was a menagerie of items that reflected and honored my life. When I lost Ramona, it became apparent to me that because she was such an integral part of my life, her fur was a necessity for my medicine bag. I immediately contacted my vet and she graciously agreed to clip some of her hair for me. This is a request that could not have been made two weeks later. After death, you have a small window to accomplish things related to your dog's body such as getting hair, taking photographs, visiting the body, retrieving any of your dog's personal items such as a collar, a blanket, etc. Do not wait, some things can be put off, but these cannot.

At a time when you can barely focus, making decisions that you can feel good about later is a challenge. No one is ever completely prepared to lose their working dog to sudden death. But take heart in the fact that there are only a few decisions that really have to be made immediately and the rest will evolve. Be gentle with yourself and those around you.

## ANTICIPATING THE LOSS – WHAT'S BEST FOR YOU AND YOUR SERVICE DOG

*It is difficult to imagine the emotional attachment a recipient has with the dog they have come to depend upon. Photo © Judith Strom.*

When someone loses their service dog suddenly, they usually say, "If only I had more time." Having time to prepare for the death of a service dog can be a blessing and a curse. News about your dog's imminent death triggers the beginning of the grief process and forces you to think about life without your partner. Anticipating the death of your dog can leave you with a sense of dread. These sentiments can interfere with your ability to enjoy what limited time you have left. You may begin feeling the loss even before your dog is gone. Long-term decisions about what is best for you and your dog must be addressed. It may be the first time that the tables are turned. Your dog has worked unconditionally for you, and now you must work to make sure his or her best interest is the number one priority.

This is the time in your relationship where the needs of the human partner conflict with the needs of the canine partner. Not only is your canine partner unable to perform, but he or she may require extensive medical care and assistance that may be difficult or impossible for you to provide. Medical expenses can be exorbitant and, depending upon your personal financial resources, may dictate some of your decision-making process.

A sick or ailing canine partner can significantly impact your independence. Not only is your dog unable to assist you in the everyday ways you have become accustomed to, but you may feel unable to leave him at home. Knowing that your faithful partner is suffering physically makes it difficult to leave him or her alone, and even when sick, working dogs do not appreciate this kind of break in routine. When my Ramona was forced into retirement, she would follow me to the back door and once the door was closed, she would howl as if to say, "Why are you leaving me? I'm supposed to go

**The loss of a service dog is much more difficult than losing a pet. It also means the loss of independence for the recipient.**

with you and you need me." Working dogs generally want to work, even when it is not in their best interest. How can you make them understand that their position in life has changed and they can no longer work? So now you have to make decisions that impede your ability to function normally and make you unpopular with your canine partner.

Take comfort. Knowing ahead of time about your service dog's retirement is a blessing as well. When Jeff found out that his assistance dog Spinner had a limited amount of time left, he was able to loosen the rules a bit and give Spinner time to relax and play in her final days. He chuckled as he recalled Spinner happily gobbling an ice cream cone. For Jeff, having time to plan gave him the crucial time needed to start thinking about and planning for a successor dog. This allowed Jeff's provider agency time to identify a successor dog. Within a month he was introduced to his new dog, Knight. Not all agencies will have a dog so readily available, so it is important to notify your agency as soon as possible so you can begin strategizing for life without a service dog and the possibility of a successor dog.

In addition to the difficulty of leaving your dog home alone, some of you will have to cope with the reality of leaving your dog in someone else's care. Whether it is due to financial reasons or agency related policy, handing your dog over is traumatic. Depending on your dog's illness, you may be unable to sustain adequate medical care for your current partner while taking on the responsibility of a successor dog. In some cases, a family member or friend may be willing to care for the dog making it easier for you to have regular contact with him

or her. In other instances, dogs are returned to the provider agency where they are adopted by a family or individual who can provide for their needs.

Even if you have all of the financial resources necessary to care for two dogs, you may not own your dog and some provider agencies have policies that prohibit you from having two working dogs within your household. Make sure you know what the agreements are between you and your provider agency and how that impacts your options. We cannot stress enough how important it is to have a good relationship with your provider agency so together you can make the best choice for everyone involved.

## EUTHANASIA

While euthanasia may be the most humane choice when a canine partner is facing a terminal condition, it can be both a beautiful and painful experience. If given enough time, you can utilize the Euthanasia Plan listed in Chapter 7 allowing you to create a setting of peace and comfort for your partner's final moments. However, all the preparation in the world will not necessarily prepare you emotionally for one of the most critical decisions you will ever have to make. Having to consider euthanasia for a service dog has the added burden of leaving you feeling powerless to help your dog the way your dog has always unconditionally helped you. Jeff described it best when he talked about his dog Spinner looking up at him as if to plead, "Help me, help me," when all there was left to do was to put Spinner out of her pain.

How do you know when it's time to euthanize your dog? We wish we could tell you there will be a lightening bolt and it will all be crystal clear. Unfortunately, life usually is not that convenient or crystal clear. And, you may not be emotionally ready when your dog is physically ready.

Guilt may be the primary emotion both immediately before and after euthanasia. Guilt is normal, but it is not helpful. You have spent your entire partnership making informed decisions about your dog. Face it, service dogs usually get more medical attention and treatment than an average pet. For dogs with pain and terminal illness, euthanasia is the culmination of your constant care and concern about your dog's wellbeing and it is an act of love.

The question you must ask yourself is, "To be there or not to be there?" This book contains interviews with multiple people who had their service dog euthanized. Each story contained its own poignant details. Euthanasia is often referred to as "putting a dog to sleep." Unfortunately, not every dog's euthanasia experience resembles gradual drifting into a blissful slumber. Final breaths and involuntary movements may vary in frequency and intensity. Whether you choose to be present or to wait nearby, we believe that it is helpful to know what to expect. Even though the details may be painful to think about, we want to give you some general things to expect so you can reduce some of your anxiety about the unknown and to help you be more prepared.

As you have already gathered, each euthanasia story is unique. You may have the burden of making painful choices, but sometimes those difficult choices are out of your control and may be made for you. The main thing we want to share with you is that euthanasia is a painful and personal experience between you, your service dog, and your vet. Rest assured your

## Questions To Ask When Considering Euthanasia

**Pain** – Is your dog experiencing constant pain?

**Mobility** – Is your dog able to move around unassisted?

**Normal Eating and Drinking** – Can your dog enjoy a meal and a dog biscuit?

**Quality of Life** – Does your dog have more bad days than good days?

**Vet's Advice** – Is your vet suggesting euthanasia at this time?

dog will now be out of pain and you can begin the active grieving process.

Make the best of the time you have left. Whether your dog requires euthanasia or dies naturally, the gift of time allows you not only to make planned decisions about his or her last days, it also gives you the opportunity to make the most of the time you have left. Take the time to play, to break the rules a little, and simply to spend quality time with your beloved partner that you will always carry with you.

## The Process Of Euthanasia May Include The Following Factors

- Administration of an oral or intravenous sedative prior to the euthanizing solution
- Physical restraints
- Varying intensity of muscle spasms or movement
- Emptying of the bowels and/or bladder
- Few last breaths following unconsciousness
- Eyes will remain open, all facial expression relaxes, the tongue may slide out of the mouth, etc.

*Kevin and his service dog Cerri speak to kids about assistance dogs. Photo Courtesy of Alicia Chatman.*

## CHAPTER NINE
# Surviving the Loss

Whether death is sudden or the inevitable consequence of a terminal illness, losing a service dog is devastating and often misunderstood. The emotions and stages of grief that are so often associated with the death of a close family member or friend are the very same emotions that recipients of service dogs feel upon the loss of their partner. Shock and disbelief, anger, guilt, depression, and eventual acceptance are common themes for all those we spoke to about the loss of their beloved service dog.

"What am I going to do?" Donna thought when she realized that Derrick, the Chocolate Lab that she depended on was no longer going to be able to help her get through her daily life.

"I just told everyone to leave me alone…It was hard, I didn't want to be bothered" was Kevin's first reaction when he lost Spanky, his Golden Retriever service dog, to liver cancer.

"I'm not ready for this," Sherry exclaimed when she was told Shep, her Springer Spaniel hearing dog, had lymphoma. Limited chemotherapy was attempted but to no avail, and after seven years of dutiful service, Shep had to be euthanized. For Sherry, "It wasn't long enough."

Elizabeth Kubler-Ross pioneered the careful examination of the grief process.

She identified common aspects for those experiencing a traumatic loss. Grieving is a very personal experience. No one should tell you how to grieve or when you should be finished grieving. Understanding that what you are feeling is normal can help you feel normal. Kubler-Ross identified the following five aspects of grief that are common to many people:

- Denial – "No not me, it can't be true"
- Anger – "Why me?"
- Bargaining – "Yes me…but"
- Depression – "Yes me"
- Acceptance – "It's ok"

There is no formula for how you will experience these aspects. Some people experience them all consecutively, while others experience them in different combinations over time. We included them only to help you realize that what you are feeling is normal.

We interviewed many service dog recipients who depended on their dogs to do everything: pulling a wheelchair, opening doors, picking up children's toys, informing them that the phone is ringing, there is someone at the door, or that it is time to get up in the morning. The absence of their service dogs created more than an emotional void, although this, too, was a very real part of their loss. It hindered or eliminated their ability to maintain the

*"We understand death for the first time when he puts his hand upon one whom we love."*
*~Madame de Stael*

> **Shock, disbelief, anger, guilt, and depression are all common emotions of those who have lost a service dog.**

routine of life that can be so healing for someone who has been traumatized. The loss of a service dog requires that the surviving partner problem-solve. How are they going to accomplish the activities of daily living and working, in addition to coping with intense emotional pain? Each grieving partner's story is unique and difficult to hear, but each holds many helpful gems of healing and remembrance.

## GETTING THROUGH THE FIRST WEEK

The first day and several days after the death of your service dog can feel excruciatingly difficult to bear. "It was like becoming disabled again and having to redefine who I was and what I could do," says Jeff regarding the loss of his service dog Spinner. Jeff, a quadriplegic, first applied for a service dog from Paws With A Cause when he was living alone and felt he needed the security when one night he awoke to an "uninvited visitor" in his home. Over the period of eleven years Jeff and Spinner fine-tuned their relationship and solidified an eternal bond. At the time of Spinner's death, Jeff had just acquired a new wheelchair and a new accessible van. These things were designed to help him make his way in the world, but Spinner, the most cherished aid to his independence, was now missing. "The first day I just sat alone at home, I didn't go to work, I just sat in the dark." Eventually, however, Jeff let practicality take over, much the way funeral and burial arrangements occupy family when a loved one dies. Jeff started to cope by "sketching out the things that needed to be done." The problems that were created by no longer having Spinner or a significant other to depend upon gave Jeff something to focus on. He was grateful to have something to do. "Luckily there were a lot of changes in my life," which gave him the incentive to regroup, reorganize and begin healing. "I started making lists, phone calls. I poured myself into shaping my life."

One of the most difficult parts of grieving is balancing the active grieving process with relief through distracting activities. Many survivors described periods of intense grief contrasted with busy activities. Sherry said about losing Shep, "I cried a lot …you know what you go through when a family member or a friend dies, it's the same damn thing." Friends helped her cope by getting her out of the house to go buy trees for a memorial garden. When he was not reorganizing his life, Jeff was looking for things to keep himself busy such as exercising, self-improvement, reading, and meditating.

When I lost Ramona, I began to make feeble attempts at coping by pouring all my pain and sorrow into a daily journal. I placed in this journal all the cards and expressions of sympathy I received. When I read that journal now, I can sense my own strength through my suffering. Each day's activity was an attempt to move toward acceptance. For instance, we made a plan to go to the vet to retrieve some of Ramona's beautiful, velvet, black hair prior to her cremation. I needed to have something of her with me. We went back a second time to get some more the following day. I felt a little crazy for doing this, but they did not question me. I will keep her hair in a medicine bag throughout my lifetime to help me heal physically and emotionally.

Working closely with the agency who supplied your dog may help alleviate some of the fears and burdens you are bearing. Many recipients worry about the cost of a successor dog since raising money can take several months. Cost varies dramatically from agency to agency, making it difficult to identify a standardized monetary amount. Some agencies do not charge a fee. Other agencies have a special fund specifically allocated for replacement dogs for those who cannot afford to be without a dog for long. These agencies are also more likely to be aware of "…the emotional baggage that goes along with losing a dog…" as one survivor put it. At a time when you may feel you have to explain your loss over and over again and still not be understood, it can be a comfort to know that there is at least one place where someone understands. Some of the recipients we interviewed talked about how agency representatives had begun to think about their successor dog even before it was obvious to them that their dog was nearing retirement or death. "They did so much for me," said Kevin about his agency's response to the death of his Golden Retriever service dog, Spanky "…everything they could possibly do."

Seek out other survivors with whom you feel comfortable sharing your experiences and feelings. This is easier for folks who live close to their provider agency because there are often many service dog owners in close proximity. We were able to obtain a list of several people who had lost different types of assistance dogs to retirement or death by simply asking for one from an assistance dog agency. Work with your agency to develop a circle of support in your area or over telephone and internet lines. Most of the people we interviewed said that it would have been helpful to talk to someone who was going through a similar experience.

## MAKING ARRANGEMENTS

As with a death of any loved one, making arrangements can provide a concrete step in your grieving process. The one decision you cannot postpone is the disposition of your dog's body. What you decide to do will be based on your personal, religious, and cultural beliefs. You can choose to do as little or as much as you would like based on your energy level, financial situation, etc. Considerations include cremation, urn selection, burial, transportation, pick-up of cremains, costs and methods of payment, etc. What you decide determines how quickly you need to make the next decision.

Choosing cremation may afford you as much time as you need to make arrangements for a ceremony or some other activity to honor your partner. However, it requires some immediate decisions such as who will do the actual cremation, how will the body be transported to the crematorium, and are you responsible for picking up the cremains or will they be delivered to you or your vet. You may choose not to receive them and to let your vet or the crematorium handle them accordingly. These may be heart-wrenching concepts and even saying the words may seem impossible while you are grieving. Planning ahead and putting your wishes in writing will save you some of this discomfort.

Selecting an urn or vessel is another potential arrangement. This can be as elaborate or as simple as you desire and can reflect the personality of your cherished partner. Often crematoriums provide a simple tin box for the cremains. Your veterinarian may be able to provide you with a few options regarding the purchase of an urn or a vessel to store the cremains.

If you wish to bury your partner, cremated or not, you may find an animal cemetery or you may prefer a location on your property that you can visit and tend to more regularly. Burial in a cemetery may require a grave marker such as a headstone or plaque. Choosing the wording for the grave marker may be another form of expressing of your love and gratitude for your partner.

Just talking about your dog as a "body" or "remains" can be devastating and hard to handle. Most people have a tendency to want what they think is the "best" for their deceased loved one. Sometimes we have a compulsion to spend more than we can afford in order to honor our partner's life and death adequately. The reality is, anything that you do from this point on is for you and your healing process. The amount of money you spend is not any indication of the amount of love and respect that you had for your service dog.

## CREATIVE HEALING

Everyone grieves. It is a universal experience. In order to heal, we have to grieve wisely, honestly and consciously. Taking an active part in your grieving process can unlock your creativity and provide an outlet for your sorrow. Creative grieving may involve quiet moments or high energy activities. Grieving is a long term process that may occupy minutes of your day or an entire weekend. Initially, you may be consumed by the ever presence of your grief. Active and creative grieving will help you to move to a place where you can have peace about the relationship with your partner. Constant avoidance of your feelings will only lead to a deeper sense of loss. In time, the feelings of sadness will come less frequently and with less intensity if you actively participate in the grief process.

The greatest examples of creative grieving comes from survivors. One idea is to create a special location for a memorial. Jim felt the best way for him to honor Thor was with a 36 foot flag pole in his front yard where he could bury his ashes. Jeff created a shrine in his dining room that consisted of Spinner's harness, leash, and a little wooden box containing a whistle and an old tennis ball. In a moment of brilliance, Jeff's parents hired an artist, while Spinner was healthy, to take pictures and to render a portrait of Spinner that is hanging in Jeff's living room to this day. A friend of mine suggested that we honor Ramona with a memory stone. We purchased quick drying cement, a plastic mold, and some plastic letters and created a beautiful memory stone for my garden. There are many creative ways to make these if you consult a hobby or garden decor book. Grieving is a personal experience and anything that you try to help you through your loss will reflect your own talents and love for your partner.

We have gathered the following list of creative activities to share with you that can help you grieve during the first week and beyond.

- Keep some of your beloved dog's hair or a plaster imprint of his footprint close to you in a special box, medicine bag, keepsake book, etc.

- Create a shrine at home using flowers, cards and other items sent by friends and family.
- Burn a candle in remembrance of your partner.
- Order flowers for your vet to thank them for taking care of your service dog.
- Write to your dog's puppy raiser and tell them about the death of your dog.
- Shop for an urn or grave marker.
- Buy a box or chest to keep treasured items (harness, leash, favorite toy).
- Take a stroll around your neighborhood to get out of the house.
- Keep a daily journal and record your experiences and feelings. Perhaps you would like to record the arrangements you have made for your dog so you can look back and reflect on the details.
- Write an article for a newsletter or newspaper about your service dog.
- Write poetry.
- Create a special place in your yard where your dog liked to play or lie under a special tree.
- Make a photo album or scrapbook of all of your favorite pictures of you and your dog.
- Make a donation to an animal foundation, service dog program, or a local animal shelter in honor of your service dog .
- Plan a ceremony or memorial service to honor her.
- Create a special shelf in your home that pays tribute to your dog.
- Have a portrait painted of your dog.
- Plant a tree or create a special garden.

## EXPLAINING THE LOSS TO OTHERS – "PETS" CAN BE A FOUR LETTER WORD

One of the most difficult tasks during the first devastating days following the loss of your canine partner is informing others. Often the well-meaning response of friends and colleagues is to recount their own loss of a cherished pet. Sometime this response makes you feel as if they are invalidating and minimizing the nature of your loss. How do you graciously tell someone that losing a service dog is nothing like losing a pet? Losing a service dog is more akin to losing a child or a loved one. Some people may be unable to understand this relationship. Spend your energy explaining what this loss means to you only to those who really need to know such as your employer, colleagues, parents, or people you just cannot avoid. These are the people that you will need for support and understanding.

You may feel that no one understands what you are going through, but be assured there are thousands of people across the United States with similar experiences. Kevin had many friends and family members who wanted to support him through the loss of Spanky. One of these friends brought him a book about losing a pet to comfort him. Kevin says, "It didn't click because it wasn't losing a family pet. Having a dog 24 hours a day, 7 days a week that is your arms and legs is not a pet! It is a devastating loss, like losing a child." In this situation, the word "pet" is definitely an offensive word.

Don't blame someone for what they do not understand. But if they are close enough to you that they need to understand what you are going through in

Those who have lost a service dog have not only lost a friend - they have lost their independence and their lifestyle, a very real part of themselves.

*Morgan retrieving hard to reach items. Photo Courtesy of Kim Alaburda.*

order to help you, then you have a right to expect them to be open to listening to what you have to say. Begin by thanking them for their gesture and then gently explain that the role your partner played in your life is very different from the role a pet plays in someone's life. You can give an example of how your dog helped you on a daily basis. Keep in mind that you can confront someone if you choose to, or you can simply say thank you and let it go. It is up to you how you choose to handle each encounter.

We encourage you to contact your provider agency and ask if there is someone you can speak to about your loss. Talking with others who have lost a canine partner and who understand your grief can help you cope. It also minimizes your need to make everyone else understand the complexity of your loss. The list of Bereavement Help Lines listed under Resources may also provide some solace.

In the beginning you may believe there is no way to get through this. Accessing the support from those around you and actively participating in the grieving process will enable you to honor your service dog and begin healing.

# CHAPTER TEN

# Successor Dog

When Ramona was forced into retirement, I did not want to even think about getting another service dog. As time when by, I could not ignore the fact that she was getting older and finally both she and I had to accept her new retirement life. Franz began to encourage me to think about getting another service dog. After months of turning down invitations and opportunities, I began to see that he was right. I did need another service dog.

I sought the advice of a friend who worked with several service dog agencies. At this point in my life, it was much more difficult for me to travel for an extended time to a training facility. My health had declined and I did not feel strong enough to travel alone. My dear friend, Natalie Sachs-Ericsson, introduced me to a wonderful program, Paws With A Cause. She explained how they would come to my home and conduct an assessment of what a dog could do for me. Then, they would train the dog and deliver him or her to my home. After delivery, a local trainer would work with us to perfect the commands before we were tested for public certification. This sounded too good to be true. But what about Ramona? How would she feel about another dog taking her place?

I contacted Paws With A Cause and requested an application. Shortly after I submitted the written application, a home visit was scheduled. Two trainers arrived one Sunday morning. They greeted Franz and me, but they also greeted Ramona and treated her like a queen. I was astounded and pleasantly surprised that a lot of their questions focused on Ramona and her comfort level with my new service dog. My fears were put to rest immediately as they talked with us about my new dog. I began to feel the hope of independence creep back into my thoughts.

Within a couple of weeks I received a letter telling me I had been approved for a Paws With A Cause service dog. Several months went by before a dog was selected for me. I was notified that he would be arriving within the next couple of months. I was elated once again. The trainers comforted me and relieved my fears about Ramona's reaction and assured me this dog was selected based on his ability to fit into our home and live side-by-side with Ramona.

The day finally came when Morgan, a regal, male Golden Retriever, arrived at our door. He immediately ran to me and jumped in my lap as if to say, "I'm home." I greeted him outside, away from Ramona's view. We then brought him in-

*"In life, what sometimes appears to be the end is really a new beginning."*
*– Unknown*

side and introduced him to Ramona. She instantly began her dominating behavior, but Morgan never flinched. It was as if he was saying, "OK, you are number one and I am number two and that is OK with me." I was amazed and relieved. Soon they were playing together as if they had known each other all of their lives. The trainers talked to me about how I could reinforce Ramona's place in our home as the alpha dog and relieve her anxieties. What a relief! It was all working too smoothly. It was just too good to be true. How could I be so lucky to have two amazing service dogs?

Over the next few weeks and months, Morgan and I met regularly with the Paws With A Cause trainer. Ramona's behavior was very interesting. All of a sudden, she stopped trying to go with me when I would leave everyday. It was as if she were thinking, "Thank goodness Morgan finally got here and I can really relax!" She seemed relieved and more tranquil now that I had Morgan with me. I think it was a relief for both of us.

## MAKING THE DECISION TO GET A SUCCESSOR DOG

The decision to get a new dog is often stressful and difficult to make. Some individuals with a disability cannot imagine living without the assistance of a service dog, while others cannot bring themselves to get a successor dog because they are not emotionally ready

for a new commitment. Making the decision to get a successor dog requires that you acknowledge the permanence of the loss of your previous dog. You are forced to realize that all the time, energy, care, and money you invested to create the symbiotic relationship you came to trust has been spent, and you must start anew. Your old dog is irreplaceable. However, because of your job, lifestyle, or disability, the fact is you must find a replacement in order to continue your normal daily routine.

Much depends on your personal situation, both emotional and financial. You may be able to create a functional scenario with help from other people and resources that will enable you to postpone the decision to get another dog until you are ready. It may take years be-

*When Marcie received Morgan as a successor dog, she was presented with him and a manual and given two weeks prior to training with instructions to "bond." Photo Courtesy of Doug Reeves.*

> It can be very difficult emotionally, and sometimes physically, to start over with a new dog.

fore you are emotionally ready for a successor, or you may decide not to get one. If possible, take your time and make whatever choice is best for you.

## A NEW DAY DAWNS - MAKING PLANS FOR A NEW SERVICE DOG

If you do decide to get a successor dog there will be many things to consider: financial commitments, your service dog provider's policies for obtaining a successor dog, timeframe and waiting periods, family impact, training schedules, adaptation of your previous dog if still living, and more. If you have kept in close contact with your provider agency regarding your retiring dog's health, retirement and/or death, they will have more time to plan for a replacement, which can significantly shorten waiting time. As we have discussed, each provider agency has policies regarding successor dogs that could impact if and when you get a new dog. If your dog is retired and living with you, some agencies will not allow you to receive a new dog until alternate placement is found for the retiree. Learn your agency's policies regarding successor dogs as early as possible. There are many assistance dog agencies throughout the country from which you can obtain a dog. Shop around and find an agency that is most compatible with your own philosophies and desires.

Financial considerations may have a significant impact on your decision-making process. Your first consideration is whether or not your agency provides a successor dog free of charge. Even if they do, there may be costs associated with training such as travel, attendant care, hotel, airfare, time away from work, etc. If your dog is retired and living with you, there are also the additional costs of vet care, food, and grooming for two dogs.

Being emotionally and financially ready, as well as having a dog trained and available for service, are factors that may not all intersect at the same time. Rarely will you be fortunate enough for all of these things to occur simultaneously. Be realistic and take the time to prioritize what you need the most rather than holding out for a best case scenario.

## THE JOYS AND SORROWS OF A NEW SERVICE DOG

Everyone we interviewed who has received a successor dog, had a difficult time making the transition. Jeff reflected, "It took about a month for me to put everything into perspective. After a month, I drove up to Grand Rapids to meet Knight. His personality was so different, and I was warned by my agency not to make comparisons between Spinner and Knight. The agency felt Knight was not very confident and needed someone who was familiar with the ropes that he could lean on. We bonded in the first week or so and have been together for several years. Spinner was a little soldier and didn't like to be hugged. Knight is a big baby. He jumps into my bed and puts his head on my shoulder. Spinner was so confident it was only at the end that she looked at me as if to say 'I need your help.' Knight says that to me all the time. It reminds me that I depend on him the way he depends on me." Jeff managed this situation by taking a little time to gain some healthy perspective. He was then able to notice the differences between Spinner and

Knight and honor them both. Perhaps for the first time Jeff realized that he and his service dog were learning from each other. He was helping Knight the same way Knight was helping him.

Kevin shared that his experience was initially quite distressing. "I didn't get to grieve over Spanky with Gerri [his successor dog] in the house. When I got the new dog, I didn't let him bond with me. I quickly came to the conclusion that I wasn't over losing Spanky. When I went for certification with Gerri, the field trainer cancelled the certification. Once I realized what I was doing, I said to myself 'I don't want to lose another dog.' I had to let [Gerri] into my life; there was nothing I could do about it." Even if you are not emotionally ready for a new dog, you may have to put your emotions aside for your own well-being. A good agency will observe how you are coping with the loss and will not just let you take home a new dog unless the relationship is working. Kevin eventually realized that he had to grieve for Spanky even with Gerri in the house, and that grieving and adapting to the replacement dog were entirely separate things.

Donna made her decision to get a successor dog when Derrick could no longer work. She thought about placing Derrick in another home, but felt he was so old that it would be too difficult for him. She chose instead to work with her son to transition Derrick to be his dog. The day Cannon, her successor dog, came home to live with them, the agency took Derrick's harness. Donna's son became Derrick's primary caregiver, and Derrick was able to remain in their home alongside Cannon. You, your family, and your service provider should all take an active part in defining the roles of the service dog and the retired dog within the household. Opening yourself up to the possibility of a successor dog may help you to face the fact that your current dog needs to be retired.

In the final analysis, the decision to get a successor dog is both practical and emotional. We hope the insights we have shared with you will help you navigate the decision-making process. Always remember: the lessons you received in your relationship with one service dog are a gift that you can share with your successor dog.

# CHAPTER ELEVEN
## Behind Every Great Service Dog is a Great Puppy Raiser

I arrived early at the airport. I was so excited about meeting Morgan's puppy raiser that I just could not stand it. I had been looking forward to this visit for five months. Was Morgan going to recognize her? Would he tell her that I make him work all the time and do not throw his ball enough? Or maybe he would tell her that I let him sleep on the bed with me. Are his nails too long? Does his breath stink? Am I a good partner? Would he want to go home with her?

These thoughts and many more were running through my head. Then a thought struck me—how wonderful it was to feel so independent driving an hour alone from our home in Santa Fe to pick someone up at the Albuquerque airport—and all because of Morgan. As Morgan and I sat watching passengers file by, I saw a woman with a Paws With A Cause T-shirt and started to move towards her. She said later that she saw the swish of a golden tail and it caught her attention. Karole greeted me with a smile and a hug and we chatted for a few moments. I asked her if she wanted to pet Morgan. She respectfully declined saying that she preferred to wait until we arrived at my house, a more relaxed location.

As we made our way to baggage claim, I was giving Morgan commands "Heel, Left, Right" and I realized he was not paying attention to her; Morgan was listening to me. My fears subsided and my confidence grew. Later Karole told me that she was pleased to see how well he was working with me in and out of elevators and moving around the airport. She was filled with a sense of pride.

Once we were settled in at home, Karole surprised me with a wonderful storybook of photos and memorabilia of Morgan's past life. Tears welled up inside as I saw a bundle of huggable roly-poly balls of fur piled up around a proud and exhausted Golden Retriever dam, Darla. It was obvious that Morgan was loved. Karole would later say, "If a puppy raiser doesn't love a puppy it doesn't grow up to be a loving dog. So there is pain involved with being a puppy raiser, but it is worth it." How true.

The best lessons Karole gave me came during our many hours of conversation and story telling. She told me how she had to discourage Morgan's unwanted behavior, about his favorite treats, the best way to groom his feet and trim his nails, and most importantly about the "Now" command. Also, Karole aired all Morgan's dirty laundry—his fetishes for wooden picture frames and tissue paper and his burning ambition to be a sled

*"He was my puppy, but he's your dog."*
*- Karole Schaufele*

dog. She confided in me that Morgan got her through some really difficult personal times and it was difficult to say goodbye to him. Karole said, "People ask me how I can raise dogs and then give them away. I have agreed to it and made the commitment; it is the natural progression of things."

The morning Karole was to leave, we sat down for our last heart-to-heart. She told me that Morgan was a wonderful puppy and that she had been afraid it would feel as though he still belonged to her. However, seeing Morgan working with me, she realized that he belonged to me. Karole said, "I was happy to see him, but I was more excited to see you. It was great meeting you and Franz and getting the chance to see Morgan work." The last thing Karole said to me as she boarded the plane was, "Morgan is a dog that I will always love, but I love him now as your dog and not as my puppy."

## PUPPY SELECTION

Potential service dog puppies come from a variety of sources. Some puppies are donated by or purchased from breeders, some service dog organizations have their own breeding programs, yet other puppies are rescued from shelters and/or humane organizations. All puppies receive temperament and medical testing to assess their personalities, overall health, and interest in working. Temperament testing may include evaluating the puppy's aggression levels, ability to recover from loud noises, responses to stressful situations, and overall personality strengths. Medical testing focuses on the solidness of the hips because hip dysplasia and weakness in the hips can seriously limit a dog's ability to perform physical tasks. Puppies that pass the initial medical and temperament evaluations usually go to live with a volunteer puppy raiser at 7-8 weeks of age. It is often recommended that rescued puppies be at least 14 months old before entering a puppy raising program and have additional temperament and medical testing because agencies are unaware of their bloodlines, treatment, and medical history.

## THE ROLE OF A PUPPY RAISER

It takes more than a solid training program to produce a service dog. Long before you begin your partnership with

*Karole Schaufele, Paws With A Cause volunteer, and a new litter of future service dogs. Courtesy of Alicia Chatman.*

Volunteers provide the love and foundational training that makes a dog into a good service animal.

your dog a tremendous amount of love, nurturing, support, and encouragement was given selflessly by a person or family known as a puppy raiser or foster family. Puppy raisers are usually volunteers who partner with service dog agencies to provide a warm, loving and stimulating home environment to puppies identified as potential service dogs. These individuals and families generously welcome a puppy into their home for approximately 15-18 months. During this time, the individuals work tirelessly to provide socialization and basic obedience training.

The criteria for becoming a puppy raiser is broad; however, there are two key components that are necessary to ensuring the successful development of a service dog. The first component begins at "home," building the puppy's self-esteem and sense of well-being. Puppy raisers are usually responsible for all veterinary care and other costs associated with raising the puppy. Puppy raisers are required to provide regular exercise for the puppy, whether it is a kennel run, an overhead trolley style tie-out, or daily walks on a leash. Most programs do not have age limitations for puppy raisers. Youth under age eighteen may be permitted to raise a puppy provided they have adequate parental support. Due to the enormous commitment of the full-time attention to this puppy, most agencies will only place one puppy in a home at a time and do not allow another dog under age one year in the home.

The second key component is an engaging social life that produces an outgoing, self-assured puppy. Puppy raisers must commit to train the puppy in basic obedience by attending basic obedience or puppy classes at least once a week. Puppy raisers must also agree to engage

*Jeni Exley at work at Craig Hospital in Denver, CO, with her Canine Companion for Independence service dog in training, Janice IV.*

the puppy in socialization activities at least three times a week. Socialization activities include numerous interactions such as riding public transportation, attending public sporting events, concerts, etc. Puppy raisers are encouraged to expose the puppies to a variety of environments including both rural and urban. The more exposure a puppy can receive the better his chances to be prepared for his new life and ensure his success as a service dog.

Paws With A Cause describes their Foster Puppy Program as "...designed to give puppies the early experience they need to be someone's reliable companion. Puppies are placed with their Foster Family until they are ready to begin formal training.... While the Foster Home will be supplied with a list of responsibilities, the most important will be providing love and care. All that is required is reliability, a willingness to learn, and the desire to help someone else."

*Teen Puppy Raiser. Courtesy of Assistance Dogs of the West.*

If you are interested in becoming a puppy raiser, we encourage you to contact some of the service dog organizations listed within the Appendix.

### CONTRIBUTING TO THE ONGOING LIFE OF YOUR SERVICE DOG

Some service dog agencies support contact between the puppy raiser and the service dog recipient while others, for various reasons, prefer to keep that informa-

Many organizations now provide wonderful programs that foster future assistance dogs.

tion confidential. A relationship with your dog's puppy raiser can afford you information about your dog that you might not be able to receive otherwise. As I discovered from Karole, Morgan had affinities and habits from puppyhood. This helped me to better understand his sometimes odd behaviors.

You may choose not to have a relationship with your puppy raiser or your agency may elect not to disclose puppy raiser information. If so, keep in mind that these volunteers have made an incredible sacrifice and an ongoing relationship may just be too painful. Regardless of whether you have a relationship with your puppy raiser, be assured that your dog came from a devoted, loving foster home.

### PRISON PUPS AND TEEN PUPPY RAISERS

Some service dogs begin their service to others before they ever learn their first command. The popularity of programs where service dogs are raised and trained by prison inmates for rehabilitation and by teens for community service is exploding. In 1981, Sister Pauline Quinn introduced the concept of Prison Dog Programs in which inmates learn how to train dogs to help others. This is according to The Land of Pure Gold Foundation. Through these types of programs, prison-hardened women and men learn how to make a commitment to a goal and work toward achieving it. The unconditional acceptance inmates experience from these dogs and the animal-human bond that is formed is transformative. Programs such as Puppies Behind Bars in New York and The National Education for Assistance Dog Services (NEADS)

Prison Pup Partnerships benefit inmates in ways that are especially important to their rehabilitation. They learn patience, what it is like to be completely responsible for a living being, how to give and receive unconditional love, and how to work as a team. According to The Land of Pure Gold Foundation, more and more prisons are inviting dogs in, not only to learn but to teach good behavior. In addition, statistics show that prison dogs experience advanced training in half the time as dogs raised in foster homes because of the greater number of contact hours the dogs receive from inmates. This enables them to be placed more quickly.

Teens learn responsibility and service to others through service dog puppy raising and training programs. Some teens initiate their participation individually or through organizations such as 4-H. Others are guided by caring adults who see the potential in both the teen and the dogs they will raise and train. Power Paws Assistance Dogs, in partnership with state, county, and local educational and juvenile justice facilities, administers the High Schooled Assistance Dogs (HS A-Dogs) project. HS A-D is a vocational/educational program designed to enhance the lives of at-risk teenagers through personal contact with assistance dogs and responsibility for their care and training. The teens benefit by learning self discipline, developing teaching skills, and becoming aware of the needs of individuals with disabilities. Research indicates that this program increased the participants self-esteem and school attendance. The gifts imparted by the service dogs they train are immeasurable.

Assistance Dogs of the West (ADW) in Santa Fe, New Mexico, has developed a one-of-a-kind training program in partnership with Desert Academy, a secondary school. For over ten years, students have spent their afternoons and/or part of their summer vacations training assistance dogs for individuals with physical, mental, and emotional disabilities. According to Jill Felice, ADW Director, the program has many benefits over conventional training programs. Students, who are often selected because of learning differences, gain skills in leadership, civic responsibility, and how to give without the expectation of receiving in return. Many students participate year after year and can earn leadership positions such as teacher's assistant and camp counselor. The training benefits the dogs in unique ways. The dogs spend their days in a working environment instead of a kennel, which reduces their stress and contributes to their adaptability. The school environment provides the opportunity for trainers to observe the dogs in action and to identify training areas that need improvement for each dog. In addition, from the onset the dogs in ADW's program learn to respond to the less authoritative voices of young people and to problem solve around each student's needs. This reduces placement issues by enabling each dog to become accustomed to individuals with little or no dog experience, as is the case for some service dog recipients. The program provides an invaluable service by training assistance dogs that are in high demand while at the same time reducing training costs and waiting time.

In 2005 ADW spearheaded a unique training program combining the expertise of an occupational therapist and an ADW dog trainer to work with adults with developmental disabilities to provide them with an opportunity to participate in the training of ADW service dogs. While the adult's learn life and vocational skills, the dogs learn to function in different environments with different people who use varying gestures, tones of voice, ways of speaking, and equipment.

These are just a few of the many programs involved.

*Ramona as a CCI puppy in training.*

# Conclusion and Reflections

Your life with your service dog, from the decision to get a dog to losing that dog at retirement or death and making the decision to get a successor dog, will be an incredible experience that will change you forever. Writing this book has been an enlightening journey that has offered us the opportunity to focus on the depths of my relationship with my service dogs and all that they have taught me. We hope it does the same for you. We were moved by each story and by the willingness of these individuals to share the poignant details of their life with a service dog and the joys and sorrows they experienced. Their wisdom and insights leave us with hope that, through the remarkable relationship with a service dog, we can become more independent and self-sufficient. Service dogs and the people who train and care for them enrich the lives of individuals with disabilities in countless and astounding ways.

We hope this book has guided you through the process of inviting a service dog into your life, caring for that dog, and discovering an abundance of joy and independence. We were inspired to write this book by Ramona and Morgan's unwavering dedication and loyalty. It is our hope that you will find strength in the experiences of others and in the fact that there are people who understand and respect the special bond between you and your service dog.

*"Grieve not, nor speak of me with tears, but laugh and talk of me as if I were beside you…I loved you so… 'twas heaven here with you."*
*– Isla Paschal Richardson*

# Bibliography

Assistance Dogs International, Inc.: Retrieved from www.adionline.org.

Assistance Dogs of the West: Retrieved from www.assistancedogsofthewest.org.

Delta Society: Retrieved from www.deltasociety.org.

Dr. Dee Blanco: Retrieved from www.drdeeblanco.com.

*Guide to Assistance Dog Laws* (1st ed.). (2005). Assistance Dogs International, Inc.

International Association of Assistance Dog Partners: Retrieved from www.iaadp.org.

Paws With A Cause: Retrieved from www.PawsWithACause.org.

Power Paws Assistance Dogs: Retrieved from www.azpowerpaws.org.

Walker, J. H. Obesity-related health problems: Retrieved from http://www.dogforme.com/pages/obesity.html.

# Training, Behavior, and Performance Standards for Assistance Dog

Assistance Dogs International, Inc. (http://www.adionline.org) has published the following minimum standards pertaining to the training of various types of assistance dogs. Refer to their website for current information.

## ADI MINIMUM STANDARDS FOR TRAINING SERVICE DOGS

These are intended to be minimum standards for all service dog centers that want to be affiliated with ADI. All centers are encouraged to strive to work at levels above the following minimums:

A minimum of one hundred twenty (120) hours of training over a period of no less than six (6) months, must take place under the supervision of a program's trainer. During that time at least thirty (30) hours of regularly scheduled training must be devoted to field trips and public exposure.

Basic obedience skills the dogs must master with voice and/or hand signals are: sit, stay come, down, heel and off leash recall.

The dog must show social behavior skills of no aggression, no inappropriate barking, no biting, no snapping/growling, no inappropriate jumping on strangers, no begging and no sniffing of people.

The service dog must be trained to perform at least three physical tasks.

The training time with the student prior to placement must be a minimum of 60 hours. This is both public and private. All graduates must be given a solid education in appropriate behavior of the team. The dog should stay as invisible as possible and not interfere with people.

The training facility must require the recipient to complete a follow-up progress report once a month for the first six months following placement. Personal contact will be done by qualified staff or program volunteer within twelve to eighteen (12-18) months of graduation and annually thereafter.

Identification of the Service Dog will be accomplished with a laminated ID card with a photo of the dog and partner and names of both recipient and dog. In public the dog must wear a harness, backpack or slicker with a logo that is clear and easy to read and identifiable as a service dog.

The staff of the training center must demonstrate knowledge of the disabilities of the clients it works with. Organizations shall make available educational material on different disabilities.

The recipient must agree to abide by the Minimum Standards for Assistance Dog Partners.

At the onset of training, every dog will be spayed or neutered and will have a thorough medical evaluation to determine that the dog does not have any physical problems that would cause difficulty for a working dog.

## ADI MINIMUM STANDARDS FOR TRAINING SERVICE DOGS TO SEIZURE RESPOND/ALERT

A Seizure Response/Alert dog is a dog trained and placed to work with an individual who has epilepsy or other seizure disorders. The dog is trained to perform a task or tasks, which benefit the recipient by alerting him/her to or by responding appropriately to seizure episodes. Programs associated with the ADI must demonstrate knowledge of seizure conditions including, but not limited to, epilepsy. The program staff must possess the ability to provide emergency first aid to students during the placement period. All centers are encouraged to strive to work at levels above the following minimums:

A minimum of one hundred twenty (120) hours of training over a period of no less than six (6) months, must take place under the supervision of a program's trainer. During that time at least thirty (30) hours of regularly scheduled training must be devoted to field trips and public exposure.

The dog must be able to perform both on and off leash obedience skills with voice and/or hand signals. These commands will include: sit, stay, come, down, and heel. Dogs must demonstrate absolute control on and off leash.

The dog must show social behavior skills of no aggression, no inappropriate barking, no biting, no snapping/growling, no inappropriate jumping on strangers, no begging, and no sniffing of people. Dogs must be unobtrusive and have good household skills.

The dog must be trained no less than one "appropriate response skill" i.e.: vocal alert, physical contact alert, activation of an emergency medical alert system, etc.

The training time with the student prior to placement must be a minimum of no less than sixty hours. Instruction must include obedience skills, proper behavior, and implementation into the home.

The training facility must require the recipient to complete a follow-up progress report once a month for the first six months following the placement. Personal contact will be done by qualified staff or program volunteer within eighteen (18) months of graduation and annually thereafter.

Identification of the Seizure Response/Alert Dog will be accomplished with a laminated ID card with a photo of the dog and partner and names of both recipient and dog. In public, the dog must wear a harness, backpack or slicker with a logo that is clear and easy to read and identifiable as a service dog.

At the onset of training, every dog will be spayed or neutered and will have a thorough medical evaluation to determine that the dog does not have any physical problems that would cause difficulty for a working dog.

It is the program's duty to educate the client to his/her responsibility to inform, in advance, their support system of the proper response to the seizure alert/response dog.

## ADI MINIMUM STANDARDS FOR TRAINING HEARING DOGS

These are intended to be minimum standards for all hearing dog centers that want to be affiliated with ADI. All centers are encouraged to strive to work at levels above the following minimums:

A minimum of three (3) months/sixty (60) hours of training must take place under the supervision of a program's trainer. During this time, at least twenty (20) hours of regularly scheduled training must be devoted to city work, obedience, and socialization training during the dog's entire training time.

Basic obedience skills the dog must master with voice and/or hand signals are: sit, stay come, down, heel, and off leash recall.

The dog must show social behavior skills of no aggression, no inappropriate barking, no biting, no snapping/growling, no inappropriate jumping on strangers, no begging, and no sniffing of people.

Sound awareness skills: Upon hearing a sound, the dog must make physical contact with the recipient and then specifically indicate or lead the person to the source of the sound. All dogs must be trained to at least three (3) sounds.

The placement of the Hearing Dog must last at least four (4) days/32 hours. By the end of the placement, the recipient will be able to correctly praise and discipline the dog, care for the dog, practice sound work with the dog, control the dog, and enforce obedience skills. During the placement, the trainer will go with the recipient and the dog to do city training and go to stores and a restaurant. Also, during the placement, the trainer, the recipient, and dog will practice sound work and obedience every day.

The training facility must require the recipient to complete a follow-up progress report once a month for the first six (6) months following the placement. Personal contact will be done by qualified staff or program volunteer within twelve to eighteen (12-18) months of graduation and annually thereafter.

Identification of the Hearing Dog and recipient will be accomplished with a laminated ID card with a photo of the dog and partner and names of both recipient and dog. The dog must wear a blaze orange collar and leash, approved by ADI, with Hearing Dog printed/stitched on it and a cape with the program's logo whenever in public.

The staff of the training center must demonstrate knowledge of deafness, deaf culture, and hearing impairment. A staff member or agent must know basic sign language. Organization shall make available educational material on different disabilities.

The recipient must agree to abide by the Minimum Standards for Assistance Dog Partners.

At the onset of training, every dog will be spayed or neutered and will have a thorough medical evaluation to determine that the dog does not have any physical problems that would cause difficulty for a working dog.

## ADI MINIMUM STANDARDS FOR TRAINING GUIDE DOGS

These are intended to be minimum standards for all Guide Dog programs that want to be affiliated with ADI. The training program must demonstrate the knowledge of blindness and working with the visually impaired and/or blind clients. All centers are encouraged to strive to work at levels above the following minimums:

Guide work training with program trainers must include a minimum of fifty (50) sessions, each session being a minimum of one hour over a period no less than four months. At least forty (40) of these sessions must be devoted to field trips and public exposure.

The dog must be able to perform on leash, basic obedience skills with voice commands; sit, stay come, down, heel, and recall.

The dog must show social behavior skills of no aggression, no nuisance barking, no biting, no snapping/growling, no jumping on or sniffing of people, no begging, and no other inappropriate social behavior.

The Guide Dog will be trained to negotiate obstacles, overhangs, barriers, street crossings, city and country work, and public transportation. Blindfold work must be included for each Guide Dog.

The training time with the student and dog must be at least twenty (20) days for the first time guide dog user and at least seven days for a successor Guide Dog user. All students will be given canine education on appropriate behavior, obedience, health care, retirement, and user responsibilities as outlined in ADI's Minimum Standards for Assistance Dog Partners. The team must demonstrate proficiency in negotiating obstacles and handling city and country traffic situations.

The training program must require the recipient to complete a follow-up progress report as established by their program and offer follow-up care as needed.

The school will provide a laminated ID card with a photo of the graduate and dog and names of both. In public, the Guide Dog will wear the program's appropriate guide harness.

The recipient must agree to abide by all user responsibilities as outlined in ADI's Minimum Standards for Assistance Dog Partners.

At the onset of training, every dog will be will have passed a thorough medical evaluation to determine that the dog does not have any physical problems that would cause difficulty for a working dog. Every dog will be spayed or neutered prior to placement.

It is the school's responsibility to inform the recipient of any special health and/or maintenance care requirements for each dog.

## ADI MINIMUM STANDARDS FOR TRAINING SOCIAL AND FACILITY DOGS

These standards are intended to be minimum standards for all Social and Facility Dog programs affiliated with ADI. A social or facility dog is a dog that is permanently placed in a home or care giving facility to provide therapeutic benefits. A trained designator/facilitator is required to oversee and supervise the activities and the care of the dog. The program must demonstrate the knowledge of the therapy program and the individual disability or the facility's capabilities of implementing the therapy program. All centers are encouraged to strive to work at levels above the following minimums:

A minimum of fifty (50) hours of training over three (3) months must take place under the supervision of the program's trainer. During that time, at least 24 hours of regularly scheduled training must be devoted to field trips and public exposure.

The dog must be able to perform basic obedience skills with voice commands and/or hand signals: sit, stay, come, down, and heel. Dogs must demonstrate control on and off lead.

The dog must show social behavior skills of no aggression, no nuisance barking, no biting, no snapping/growling, no jumping on strangers, no begging, and no sniffing of people. Dogs must be unobtrusive and have good household skills.

The social or facility dog may be trained for an individual or care facility. The care facility must provide at least one (1) care provider during training.

The training time with the student and/or facilitator must be a minimum of five (5) days, instruction will include obedience skills, proper behavior and implementation into the home or facility.

The training program must require the recipient to complete the follow-up progress reports as established by their program.

Social dog and Facility dog access is not recognized as canine assistance under the ADI guidelines. ID and equipment is not necessary, but may be issued at program's discretion if access laws are understood by the individual and/or facility.

The recipient must agree to abide by all user responsibilities.

Prior to completion of training, each dog will be spayed or neutered and will have passed a thorough medical evaluation to determine that the dog does not have any physical problems that would cause difficulty for a dog's working role.

# Appendix II

# Assistance Dog Resources

We have compiled a list of publications and websites that we believe might be helpful to you as you embark on your personal journey of pursuing, caring for, and living with a service dog.

## BOOKS, POEMS, AND PUBLICATIONS

*Animal Helpers for the Disabled,* Deborah Kent, Watts Library, 2006. A clear, easy-to-read book on dogs that help people, for grade school children.

*Helping Paws: Dogs That Serve,* Melinda Luke, Marcy Dunn Ramsey, Cartwheel, 2002. Describes all types of working and service dogs, for children ages 4-8.

*Dr. Pitcairn's Complete Guide to Natural Health for Dogs & Cats,* Dr. Richard H. Pitcairn, DVM and Ph.D. and Susan Hubble Pitcairn, Rodale Press, Inc., 1995.

*First Aid for Dogs: What to Do When Emergencies Happen,* Bruce Fogle, DVM, Penguin Books, 1995.

*Getting in Touch with Your Dog,* Linda Tellington-Jones, Trafalgar Square Publishing, 1999.

*Holistic Guide for a Healthy Dog,* Wendy Volhard, Kerry Brown, Howell Book House, 2nd edition, 2000. Natural diets and natural ways to keep your dog healthy.

*I'll Always Love You,* Hans Wilhelm, Crown Publishers Inc., 1985. Children's book that portrays the close relationships between a boy and his dog and is comforting during the loss of a dog.

*Love Heels,* Patricia Dibsie, Yorkville Press, 2003. Stories and photographs about Canine Companions for Independence.

*Service Dogs (Dog Heroes),* Linda Tagliaferro, Wilma Melville, Bearport Publishing 2005. A book for children ages 9-12.

## INTERNET WEBSITES

**American Dog Trainers Network;** http://www.inch.com/~dogs/service.html, a listing of service dog trainers throughout the U.S. by state.

**American Kennel Club:** http://www.akc.org, Extensive website on AKC registered dog breeds, dog registrations, shows, events and other dog related subjects.

**Assistance Dog Institute:** http://www.assistancedog.org/, 215 Sebastopol Rd., Santa Rosa, CA 95407, Phone: (707) 545-DOGS (3647), Fax: (707) 585-0800, offers Associate of Science degree programs in Assistance Dog Education and Human-Canine Life Sciences. These programs teach people how to select, train, and place service dogs, along with all the business aspects of setting up a service dog agency.

**Assistance Dog United Campaign** (ADUC): http://www.assistancedogunitedcampaign.org, a health and human welfare organization which provides financial assistance to individuals who have the need for an assistance dog but have difficulty in raising the necessary funds.

**Assistance Dogs International Inc.** (ADI): http://www.adionline.org, a coalition of not-for-profit organizations that train and place assistance dogs.

**Delta Society®:** 875 - 124th Ave NE, Ste 101, Bellevue, WA 98005
Phone: 425-679-5500
Fax: 425-679-5539 www.deltasociety.org, an extensive organization dedicated to improving human health through service and therapy animals. Information and referral center.

**Disability Resource Directory:** http://www.disability-resource.com/service-dogs.html, lists many resources of interest.

**International Association of Assistance Dog Partners** (IAADP): http://www.iaadp.org, PO Box 1326, Sterling Heights, MI 48311, Phone: 810-826-3938. This non-profit cross disability organization represents people partnered with guide, hearing and service dogs. Offers resources, advocacy, veterinary care partnerships programs and an outreach and educational project for veterinary schools.

**International Society of Canine Cosmetologists:** http://www.petstylist.com, explains certification and provides information on selecting a groomer.

**Los Animales Holistic Veterinary Care and Education:** http://www.drdeeblanco.com, Dr. Dee Blanco's holistic veterinary care and education site.

**Operant Conditioning Training:** http://groups.yahoo.com/group/OC-Assist-Dogs. List with emphasis on positive reinforcement (clicker training) for Assistance Dogs (Service Dogs), an interactive online email list for service dog recipients and trainers.

**Psychiatric Service Dog Society** (PSDS): http://www.psychdog.org, dedicated to responsible Psychiatric Service Dog (PSD) education, advocacy, research and training facilitation.

**The Land of Pure Gold Foundation:** http://www.landofpuregold.com, a non-profit organization devoted to championing the human-canine bond.

**Therapy Dogs International, Inc.** http://www.tdi-dog.org, a non-profit volunteer organization dedicated to regulating, testing, and registration of therapy dogs and their volunteer handlers for the purpose of visiting nursing homes, hospitals, and other institutions.

**Veterinary Information for Dog Owners:** www.vetinfo.com/doginfo.html, a resource for dog owners seeking health and medical information.

**Working Like Dogs:** http://www.workinglike-dogs.com, a resource for people around the world with working dogs and service dogs.

## INTERNATIONAL TRAVEL REQUIREMENTS

**Canadian Embassy:**
http://www.canadianembassy.org

**European Union Member States:** http://europa.eu/abc/travel/pets/index_en.htm

**Mexican Embassy** (English):
http://www.embassyofmexico.org/eng/

**United States Department of Agriculture /APHIS:**
http://www.aphis.usda.gov/ac/pettravel.html

**United States Department of Homeland Security Transportation Security Administration:** www.tsa.gov

## HOUSING AND LEGAL ADVICE

**Assistance Dogs International,** *Guide to Assistance Dog Laws and Legal Rights of Guide Dogs*

*and Assistance Dogs:* www.adionline.org

**Americans with Disabilities Act** (ADA) Documents Center: www.iaadp.org/doglaws

**ADA Home Page:** www.ada.gov, provides legal information on the Americans with Disabilities Act.

**U.S. Department of Justice, Americans with Disabilities Act** (ADA): http://www.usdoj.gov/crt/ada

**U.S. Department of Housing and Urban Development,** Office of Fair Housing and Equal Opportunity: http://www.hud.gov/offices/fheo/library/huddojstatement.pdf

**Service Animals in Housing:** www.deltasociety.org

## DOG SUPPLY COMPANIES

**1-800 Pet Meds**
- Address: 1441 SW 29th Ave., Pompano Beach, FL 33069
- Phone: (800) 738-6337
- Pharmacy Faxline: (800) 600-8285
- Website: http://www.1800PetMeds.com
- Services Provided: online pharmacy for medications and pet supplies

**Backcountry Edge, Inc.**
- Address: 708 Ditz Dr., Manheim, PA 17545
- Phone: (717) 665-1576 or (800) 617-0643
- Fax: (717) 665-0880
- Website: http://www.backcountryedge.com
- Services Provided: supplier of outdoor canine gear, etc.

**Care-A-Lot Pet Supply**
- Address: 1617 Diamond Springs Rd., Virginia Beach, VA 23455
- Phone: (757) 460-9771
- Fax: (866) 379-3604
- Website: http://www.carealotpets.com
- Services Provided: pet supply catalog

**Dogs in Motion**
- Address: 5503 W 8000N Rd., Manteno, IL 60950
- Phone and Fax: (815) 468-0157
- Website: https://www.dogs-in-motion.com
- Services Provided: quality service dog support harnesses

**Drs. Foster and Smith**
- Phone: (800) 381-7179
- Website: http://www.drsforstersmith.com
- Services Provided: online and catalog supplier of pet products and equipment

**J B Wholesale Pet Supply**
- Address: 5 Raritan Rd., Oakland, NJ 07436
- Phone: (800) 526-0388
- Fax: (800) 788-5005
- Website: http://www.jbpet.com
- Services Provided: full service pet supply catalog

**Hearing Impaired.net**
- Website: http://www.mrpaws.com
- Services Provided: vests, insignias, ID patches for service and hearing dogs

**Kings Valley Collies Service Dog Equipment**
- Address: 39968 Ward Rd., Kings Valley, OR 97361
- Phone: (541) 929-2100
- Website: http://www.Kingsvalleycollies.com
- Services Provided: backpacks and other equipment for service and mobility dogs

**LoneWolf Dogwear**
- Address: 1201 N. Spring St., New Ulm, MN, 56073-1131
- Phone: (507) 359-9519
- Fax: (507) 359-5574
- Website: http://www.lonewolfdogwear.com Services: dog vests for service, guide, medical alert and therapy dogs

### Nu-Capes

- Address: P.O. Box 52648, Philadelphia, PA 19115
- Phone and Fax: (215) 552-9488
- Website: http://www.nucapes.com
- Services Provided: offers reflective identification capes and accessories for working dogs

### Pet Edge

- Address: P.O. Box 128, Topsfield, MA 01983-0228
- Phone: (800) 738-3343
- Fax: (800) 329-6372
- Website: http://www.petedge.com
- Services Provided: pet supplies

### PetGuys.com

- Address: 3535 Hollis St., Building B, Oakland, CA 94608
- Phone: (800) 360-4144 or (510) 547-5754
- Website: http://www.petguys.com
- Services Provided: online canine supply retail store

### SitStay.com

- Address: 5831 N 58th St., Lincoln, NE 68507
- Phone: 800-SITSTAY (800-748-7829) or (402) 467-3426
- Fax: (402) 467-5055
- Website: http://www.sitstay.com
- Services Provided: online canine supply retail store

### SmartPak

- Address: 40 Grissom Rd, Suite 500, Plymouth, MA 02360
- Phone: (800) 326-0282
- Fax: (774) 773-1444
- Website: http://www.smartpakcanine.com
- Services Provided: online canine supply retail store

### Wolf Packs, Inc.

- Address: P.O. Box 3195, Ashland, OR 97520
- Phone: (541) 482-7669
- Website: http://www.wolfpacks.com
- Services Provided: manufacturer of backpacks and other outdoor equipment

## BEREAVEMENT HELP LINES

*Cornell University Pet Loss Support Hotline:* (607) 253-3932
*Michigan State University Pet Loss Support Hotline:* (517) 432-2696
*Pet Bereavement Counseling:* www.petloss.org
*The Ohio State University Companion Animal Listening Line:* (614) 292-1823
*Tufts University Pet Loss Hotline:* (508) 839-7966
*Virginia-Maryland Regional College of Veterinary Medicine Pet Loss Hotline:* (540) 231-8038

Many more references can be found on the Delta Society and Assistance Dogs International websites.

## SERVICE DOG TRAINERS AND TRAINING PROGRAMS

Please Note: Neither the authors nor the publisher endorse, approve, or recommend these sources and omissions do not in any way indicate bias on the part of the authors or publisher. This list is supplied solely as a resource for the reader to investigate and is not intended to be exhaustive nor all-inclusive. Agencies, organizations and suppliers change and form on a continual basis. Please use this list as a starting place for your own research.

The following list was provided by the Delta Society.

**All Purpose Canines**

- Address: P.O. Box 214,
  Aberdeen, SD 57402-0214
- Phone: (605) 225-1131
- Fax: (605) 225-1131
- Website: http://www.allpurposecanines.com
- Types of Animals Trained: Hearing, Mobility, Psychiatric
- Services Provided: multiple disabilities, own animal, train handler, take donations, test and provide ID, children (6 yrs., based on maturity of child)
- Comments: Provides services nationally and internationally.

**America's Best Companions Service Dogs International**

- Address: 74682 Yucca Tree,
  Palm Desert, CA 92260
- Phone: (760) 568-6475
- Types of Animals Trained: Mobility
- Services Provided: own animal, train handler, take donations, test and provide ID
- Comments: Provides services nationally and in Canada, United Kingdom, Australia, and New Zealand.

**Assistance Dogs For Living**

- Address: 5604 Kerth Rd.,
  St. Louis, MO 63128
- Phone: (314) 892-0574
- Fax: (314) 892-0574
- Website: http://www.marilynpona.com
- Types of Animals Trained: Guide, Hearing, Mobility, Seizure, Psychiatric, Other
- Services Provided: multiple disabilities, own animal, train handler, test and provide ID, apprenticeship, children.
- Comments: Provides services nationally and internationally. Also trains dogs for Diabetes alert.

**Assistance Dogs Of The West**

- Address: P.O. Box 31027,
  Santa Fe, NM 87594
- Phone: (505) 986-9748
- Website: http://assistancedogsofthewest.org
- Types of Animals Trained: Hearing, Mobility, Psychiatric
- Services Provided: own animal, take donations, test and provide ID, children (based on maturity of child)
- Comments: Provides services nationally.

**Bob Roberto Training**

- Address: 186 Fawn Dr.,
  Guffey, CO 80820
- Phone: (719) 479-4142
- Types of Animals Trained: Guide, Hearing, Mobility, Seizure
- Services Provided: multiple disabilities, own animal, train handler, take donations, test and provide ID, apprenticeship, children (based on maturity of child)
- Comments: Provides services nationally.

**Canine Assistants, Inc.**

- Address: 3160 Francis Rd.,
  Alpharetta, GA 30004
- Phone: (770) 664-7178
- Fax: (770) 664-7820
- Website: http://www.canineassistants.org
- Types of Animals Trained: Mobility, Seizure, Hearing
- Services Provided: multiple disabilities, children (based on maturity of child)
- Comments: Provides services nationally.

**Canine Helpers For The Handicapped, Inc.**

- Address: 5699 Ridge Rd.,
  Lockport, NY 14094
- Phone: (716) 433-4035
- Fax: (716) 433-4035
- TDD: (716) 433-4035
- Website: caninehelpers.netfirms.com

- Types of Animals Trained: Guide, Hearing, Mobility, Seizure, Psychiatric
- Services Provided: multiple disabilities, own animal, train handler, take donations, test and provide ID, apprenticeship, children (6 yrs., based on maturity of child)
- Comments: Provides services nationally and internationally. Also provides memorial gardens for those who wish to honor a canine helper.

### Canine Help of ZORRO's Dynasty

- Address: P.O. Box 10182, Blacksburg, VA 24062-0182
- Phone: (540) 268-1331
- Website: http://www.ofzorrosdynastychows.com
- Types of Animals Trained: Mobility, Seizure, Psychiatric
- Services Provided: multiple disabilities, test and provide ID, help select, children (based on the maturity of the child)
- Comments: Trains dogs. Trains nationally. Scheduling is severely limited. Can only take clients who are flexible in scheduling and able to travel to Virginia.

### Canine Support Teams, Inc.

- Address: P.O. Box 956, Galt, CA 95632-0956
- Phone: (209) 745-3701
- Fax: (209) 745-3007
- TDD: Use a relay service.
- Website: http://www.caninesupportteams.org
- Types of Animals Trained: Mobility, Hearing
- Services Provided: multiple disabilities, train handler, take donations, children (8 yrs, based on maturity of child)
- Comments: Provides services nationally and internationally provided individual is able to travel to Canine Support Teams.

### Capable Canines of Wisconsin

- Address: 1905 Miller St. Apt. 25, La Crosse, WI. 54601
- Phone: (608) 796-0260
- Fax: (608) 796-0502
- Website: http://www.capablecanineswi.com
- Types of Animals Trained: Mobility
- Services Provided: multiple disabilities, own animal, take donations, test and provide ID, children (based on maturity of child)
- Comments: Provides services nationally.

### Carolina Canines for Service, Inc.

- Address: P.O. Box 12643, Wilmington, NC 28405
- Phone: (910) 362-8181
- Fax: (910) 362-8184
- Website: http://www.carolinacanines.org
- Types of Animals Trained: Mobility
- Services Provided: multiple disabilities, take donations, test and provide ID, children (based on maturity of child)
- Comments: Provides services nationally. Facility located at 1200 N. 23rd Street, Suite 101, Wilmington, NC 28405.

### CARES, Inc.

- Address: P.O. Box 314, Concordia, KS 66901-0314
- Phone: (785) 243-1077 or (800) 498-1077
- Fax: (785) 243-1079
- Types of Animals Trained: Hearing, Mobility. Seizure, Psychiatric
- Services Provided: multiple disabilities, own animal, train handler, take donations, test and provide ID, apprenticeship, children (based on maturity of child)
- Comments: Provides services nationally, Canada, and Mexico.

### Comprehensive Pet Therapy, Inc.

- Address: 7274 Roswell Rd., Atlanta, GA 30328
- Phone: (770) 396-6433

- Fax: (770) 396-6899
- Website: http://www.cpt-training.com
- Types of Animals Trained: Hearing, Mobility, Psychiatric
- Services Provided: multiple disabilities, own animal, train handler, test and provide ID, apprenticeship, children (based on maturity of child)
- Comments: Provides services nationally.

**Cosby's Therapy Animals, Inc.**
- Address: P.O. Box 7837,
  Marietta, GA 30065-1837
- Phone: (770) 735-3828
- Fax: (770) 735-3828
- TDD: (770) 735-3828
- Types of Animals Trained: Mobility, Psychiatric
- Services Provided: multiple disabilities, own animal, test and provide ID, children (based on maturity of child)
- Comments: Places dogs nationally and internationally. Every situation receives individual consideration.

**Doggie Do Good**
- Address: 514 E. San Luis Drive,
  Santa Maria, CA 93455
- Phone: (805) 896-2344
- Phone (Toll Free): (877) K9RULES
- Fax: (805) 938-1274
- Website: http://www.doggiedogood.com
- Types of Animals Trained: Hearing, Mobility, Psychiatric
- Services Provided: multiple disabilities, train own animal, train handler, apprenticeship, help select, children
- Comments: Trains dogs, cats and other species. Trains nationally.

**Dogshelp**
- Address: 401 Labore Rd., #115,
  Little Canada, MN 55117
- Phone: (651) 484-6257, voice mailbox #67951

- Types of Animals Trained: Hearing, Mobility, Seizure, Psychiatric, Other
- Services Provided: multiple disabilities, own animal, train handler, take donations, test and provide ID, apprenticeship, children (8 yrs.)
- Comments: Provides services nationally and internationally. Recipient must participate in 12 or 16 week course. Animals trained by handlers who have disabilities. Techniques are positive; no force. Also trains dogs for social therapy for Alzheimer and brain stem injuries.

**Endless Pawsabilities of Arkansas**
- Address: 513 West Ashley St.,
  Benton, AR 72015
- Phone: (501) 944-6086
- Website: http://www.endlesspawsabilities.bizhosting.com
- Types of Animals Trained: Hearing
- Services Provided: multiple disabilities, own animal, train handler, take donations, test and provide ID, help select, children (based on maturity of the child)
- Comments: Provides services nationally. Also offers therapy dog certification and training.

**Eye Dog Foundation**
- Address: 8252 S. 15th Ave.,
  Phoenix, AZ 85041
- Phone: (602) 276-0051 or (800) 393-3641
- Fax: (602) 276-1046
- Website: http://www.eyedogfoundation.org
- Types of Animals Trained: Guide
- Services Provided: take donations
- Comments: Provides services nationally and internationally.

**Georgia Canines for Independence**
- Address: 6683 Bells Ferry Road, Suite H,
  Woodstock, GA 30189
- Phone: (770) 926-0003
- Fax: (770) 926-0003

- Website: http://www.gcidogs.org
- Types of Animals Trained: Mobility, Seizure, Psychiatric
- Services Provided: multiple disabilities, children (based on maturity of child)
- Comments: Places dogs nationally.

**The Gift of Sunshine, Inc.**
- Address: 1940 Stonesthrow Rd., Bethlehem, PA 18015
- Phone: (610) 554-8725
- Website: http://www.thegiftofsunshine.org
- Types of Animals Trained: Mobility, Other
- Services Provided: multiple disabilities, own animal, take donations, test and provide ID, children (based on maturity of child)
- Comments: Provides services nationally. Helped develop the Parkinson's Walker Dog program at Independence Dogs, Inc. Continues to train Parkinson's Walker Dogs.

**Great Plains Assistance Dogs Foundation**
- Address: 920 Short St., Jud, ND 58454
- Phone: (877) 737-8364
- Fax: (701) 685-2290
- Website: http://www.greatplainsdogs.com
- Types of Animals Trained: Hearing, Mobility, Seizure, Psychiatric
- Services Provided: multiple disabilities, own animal, train handler, take donations, test and provide ID, apprenticeship, children (based on maturity of child)
- Comments: Services available are individualized. Provides services nationally and in Canada. Cross-training.

**Guide Dog Foundation For The Blind, Inc.**
- Address: 371 East Jericho Turnpike, Smithtown, NY 11787
- Phone: (800) 548-4337 or (631) 930-9000
- Fax: (631) 930-9009
- Website: http://www.guidedog.org

- Types of Animals Trained: Guide
- Services Provided: take donations, children (14 yrs., based on maturity of child)
- Comments: Provides services nationally and in Brazil, Canada, Israel, and Mexico.

**Guide Dogs for the Blind, Inc.**
- Address: 350 Los Ranchitos Rd., San Rafael, CA 94903
- Phone: (415) 499-4000 or (800) 295-4050
- Fax: (415) 499-4035
- Website: http://www.guidedogs.com
- Types of Animals Trained: Guide
- Comments: Provides services nationally and in Canada.

**Guiding Eyes For The Blind**
- Address: 611 Granite Springs Rd., Yorktown Heights, NY 10598
- Phone: (914) 245-4024 or (800) 942-0149
- TDD: (800) 421-1220
- Fax: (914) 245-1609
- Website: http://www.guidingeyes.org
- Types of Animals Trained: Guide
- Services Provided: children (16 yrs., based on maturity of child)
- Comments: Provides services nationally and in Bermuda, Canada, France, Germany, Israel, Mexico, Philippines, Puerto Rico, South America, and Switzerland.

**Heaven Scent Paws, Inc.**
- Address: 108 PP Highway, St. Elizabeth, MO 65075
- Phone: (573) 493-2627
- Fax: (573) 493-2627
- Website: http://www.heavenscentpaws.com
- Types of Animals Trained: Seizure, Diabetes/Hypoglycemia
- Services Provided: multiple disabilities, own animal, take donations, test and provide ID, apprenticeship, help select, children (based on maturity of the child)
- Comments: Trains dogs. Trains nationally

and internationally (Canada, Australia, and Great Britain).

## HELPERDOGS Training and Equipment

- Address: P.O. Box 7724,
  Wilmington, DE 19803-0724
- Website: http://www.helperdogs.us
- Types of Animals Trained: Mobility, Psychiatric
- Services Provided: multiple disabilities, own animal, train handler, donations, children (based on maturity of child)
- Comments: Provides services nationally. For owners/trainers too far to travel for training sessions, will consult and guide via AOL instant messaging, ICQ, email, or phone.

## Institute of Rural Health/Idaho State Univ.

- Address: Campus Box 8174,
  Idaho State University, Pocatello, ID 83209
- Phone: (208) 282-4436
- Website: http://www.isu.edu
- Services Provided: own animal, train handler, help select, children
- Comments: Trains nationally. Trains dogs to work with brain injury to assist with orientation to time and place. Works with people with disabilities to improve human-animal bond and to support owner training of service animals.

## International Hearing Dogs, Inc.

- Address: 5901 E. 89th Ave.,
  Henderson, CO 80640
- Phone: (303) 287-3277
- TDD: (303) 287-3277
- Fax: (303) 287-3425
- Website: http://www.pawsforsilence.org
- Types of Animals Trained: Guide, Hearing
- Services Provided: multiple disabilities
- Comments: Provides services nationally and in Canada.

## KSDS, Inc. (No Longer Listed as Kansas Specialty Dog Service)

- Address: 124 West 7th St.,
  Washington, KS 66968
- Phone: (785) 325-2256
- Fax: (785) 325-2258
- Website: http://www.ksds.org
- Types of Animals Trained: Guide, Mobility
- Services Provided: children (based on maturity of child)
- Comments: Provides services nationally and will consider international.

## Kings Valley Collies Service Dogs & Equipment

- Address: 39968 Ward Rd.,
  Kings Valley, OR 97361
- Phone: (541) 929-2100
- Fax: (541) 929-4593
- Website:
  http://www.Kingsvalleycollies.com
- Types of Animals Trained: Hearing, Mobility, Other
- Services Provided: multiple disabilities, own animal, train handler, take donations, test and provide ID, apprenticeship, children (12 yrs., based on maturity of child)
- Comments: Provides services nationally and internationally as long as no language barrier. Custom training with individual consideration. Team training required in Oregon. Also trains dogs for stroke.

## Leader Dogs For The Blind

- Address: 1039 S. Rochester Rd.,
  Rochester, MI 48308
- Phone: (248) 651-9011 or (888) 777-5332
- TTY: (248) 651-3713
- Fax: (248) 651-5812
- Website: http://www.Leaderdog.org
- Types of Animals Trained: Guide
- Services Provided: multiple disabilities, take donations
- Comments: Provides services nationally and internationally.

**Lost Acres Assistance Dogs**

- Address: Rt. 4 Box 643, Marble Hill, MO 63764
- Phone: (573) 238-3049
- Website: http://lostacresassistancedogs.bravehost.com
- Types of Animals Trained: Mobility, Psychiatric, Hearing, Medical Alert, Seizure Response, Guide, Birth Defects, and Delayed Development
- Services Provided: multiple disabilities, own animal, train handler, test and provide ID, help select, children (based on the maturity of the child)
- Comments: Places dogs throughout U.S., not a 501(c)3, internships for 18 years and older.

**Loving Paws Assistance Dogs**

- Address: P.O. Box 12005, Santa Rosa, CA 95406-2005
- Phone: (707) 569-7092
- Fax: (707) 569-7270
- Website: http://www.lovingpaws.com
- Types of Animals Trained: Mobility
- Services Provided: take donations, children (5-17 yrs., based on maturity of child)
- Comments: Provides services nationally.

**Midwest Assistance Dogs, Inc.**

- Address: P.O. Box 1891, South Bend, IN 46634
- Phone: (574) 272-7677
- TDD: (574) 287-7677
- Website: http://www.midwestassistance-dogs.org
- Types of Animals Trained: Hearing, Mobility, Seizure, Psychiatric, Other
- Services Provided: multiple disabilities, own animal, test and provide ID, children (based on maturity of child)
- Comments: Provides services nationally. Also trains therapy dogs for therapeutic intervention and companion dogs for individuals interested in the companionship of a pre-trained dog.

**National Education Of Assistance Dog Services, Inc. (NEADS)**

- Address: P.O. Box 213, West Boylston, MA 01583
- Phone: (978) 422-9064
- TDD: (978) 422-9064
- Fax: (978) 422-3255
- Website: http://www.neads.org
- Types of Animals Trained: Hearing, Mobility, Other.
- Services Provided: multiple disabilities, own animal, take donations, apprenticeship, children (based on maturity of child)
- Comments: Provides services nationally. Also trains social dogs for children

**National Service Dogs**

- Address: P.O. Box 28009, Preston Postal Outlet; Cambridge, Ontario; Canada N3H-5N4
- Phone: (519) 623-4188
- Fax: (519) 623-9997
- Website: http://www.nsd.on.ca
- Types of Animals Trained: Guide, Mobility, Psychiatric, Other
- Services Provided: multiple disabilities, take donations, apprenticeship, children (4 yrs., based on maturity of the child)
- Comments: Provides services in Canada and the United States. Our main program is training service dogs for children with autism.

**New Life Mobility Assistance Dogs**

- Address: 206 Cherry St., Wilkesboro, NC 28697
- Phone: (336) 838-2215
- Website: http://nlmad.org
- Types of Animals Trained: Mobility
- Services Provided: multiple disabilities, train handler, take donations, test and provide ID, children (8 yrs, based on maturity of child)

- Comments: Provides services nationally. Most of the service dogs trained have been selected from local animal shelters.

## Okada Specialty Guide Dogs

- Address: 7509 E. Saviors Path, Floral City, FL 34436
- Phone: (540) 635-3937
- TDD: Relay System
- Website: http://www.okadadogs.com
- Types of Animals Trained: Hearing, Guide, Seizure, Other
- Services Provided: take donations, apprenticeship, children
- Comments: Provides services nationally. Also trains Alzheimer's, residential therapy, visiting therapy, companion, and Happy Hound (a canine for kids with cancer). Also participates in educational public speaking events. Okada is a 501(c)(3) non-profit organization. $50 application fee; once accepted into the program, all training for the human partner and the dog is free to the recipient.

## Paws With A Cause® - National Headquarters

- Address: 4646 South Division, Wayland, MI 49348
- Phone: (800) 253-7297
- TDD: (800) 253-7297
- Fax: (616) 877-0248
- Website: http://www.pawswithacause.org
- Types of Animals Trained: Hearing, Mobility, Seizure
- Services Provided: multiple disabilities, own animal, take donations, apprenticeship, children (14yrs., based on maturity of child)
- Comments: Provides services nationally.

## Paws-Up, Inc.

- Address: P.O. Box 1008, Derby, KS 67037
- Phone: (316) 789-9196
- Website: http://www.paws-up.net

- Types of Animals Trained: Hearing, Mobility, Seizure, Other
- Services Provided: multiple disabilities, train handler, take donations, apprenticeship, children (based on maturity of child)
- Comments: Provides services nationally.

## Pilot Dogs, Inc.

- Address: 625 W. Town St., Columbus, OH 43215
- Phone: (614) 221-6367
- Fax: (614) 221-1577
- Website: http://www.PilotDogs.org
- Types of Animals Trained: Guide
- Services Provided: multiple disabilities, take donations, children (15 yrs., based on maturity of child)
- Comments: Provides services nationally and in Argentina, Canada, Israel, and Russia.

## Pro-Train

- Address: 1544 Avohill Drive, Vista, CA 92084
- Phone: (760) 749-0897 or (877) 223-3647 (toll-free)
- Website: http://www.protraindog.com
- Types of Animals Trained: Guide, Hearing, Mobility, Psychiatric, Other
- Services Provided: multiple disabilities, own animal, apprenticeship, children (based on maturity of child)
- Comments: Provides services nationally. Also train Protection dogs.

## Puppies Behind Bars, Inc.

- Address: 10 East 40th Street, 19th Floor, New York, NY 10016
- Phone: (212) 680-9562
- Fax: (212) 689-9330
- Website: http://www.puppiesbehindbars.com
- Types of Animals Trained: Guide
- Services Provided: children (based on maturity of child).

- Comments: Provides services nationally and in Canada and France.

**Rocky Mountain Command Dogs**
- Address: 3240 Linney Rd., Bozeman, MT 59718
- Phone: (406) 388-1197
- Website: http://www.rmcdi.com
- Types of Animals Trained: Guide, Hearing, Mobility, Seizure, Psychiatric, Other
- Services Provided: multiple disabilities, own animal, train handler, take donations, test and provide ID, apprenticeship, help select, children (12 yrs., based on maturity of child)
- Comments: Provides services nationally and internationally. Also trains cancer detection/medical service dogs.

**SAR Unit, Inc.**
- Address: 813 Hwy 1, Murray, NE 68409
- Phone: (402) 978-8889
- Fax: (402) 235-3148
- Website: http://www.sarunitinc.org
- Types of Animals Trained: Hearing, Mobility, Psychiatric, Other
- Services Provided: multiple disabilities, own animal, take donations, test and provide ID, children (8 yrs., based on maturity of child)
- Comments: Trains with individuals privately. Provides services nationally. Also trains social therapy and hospice dogs.

**The Seeing Eye**
- Address: P.O. Box 375, Morristown, NJ 07963-0375
- Phone: (973) 539-4425
- Fax: (973) 539-0922
- Website: http://www.seeingeye.org
- Types of Animals Trained: Guide
- Services Provided: children (16 yrs.)
- Comments: Provides services nationally and Canada.

**Southeastern Guide Dogs, Inc.**
- Address: 4210 77th St. E., Palmetto, FL 34221
- Phone: (941) 729-5665 or (800) 944-DOGS
- Fax: (941) 729-6646
- Website: http://www.guidedogs.org
- Types of Animals Trained: Guide
- Services Provided: multiple disabilities (for the blind with another disability)
- Comments: Provides services nationally and internationally.

**StarLight Assistance Animal Academy and Training Center**
- Address: P.O. Box 1026, Columbia, LA 71418-1026
- Phone: (318) 649-7880
- Website: http://www.starlightassistanceanimals.org
- Types of Animals Trained: Hearing, Mobility, Seizures
- Services Provided: multiple disabilities, own animal, train handler, test and provide ID, children (6 yrs., based on maturity of child)
- Comments: Provides services nationally. Also provides Internet training.

**Sterling Service Dogs©**
- Address: 5440 Brookdale, Broomfield Hills, MI 48304
- Phone: (586) 977-9716
- Fax: (586) 977-0079
- Types of Animals Trained: Mobility
- Services Provided: own animal, train handler, take donations, test and provide ID
- Comments: Provides service nationally.

**Support Dogs, Inc.**
- Address: 11645 Lilburn Park Ave., St. Louis, MO 63146
- Phone: (314) 997-2325
- Fax: (314) 997-7202
- Website: http://www.supportdogs.org

- Types of Animals Trained: Mobility
- Services Provided: multiple disabilities, train handler, take donations, apprenticeship, children (based on maturity of child)
- Comments: Train and place service dogs with adults and children who have physical disabilities at no charge. Also train and certify therapy dog teams (people and their own dogs) to visit hospitals, nursing homes, and rehabilitation centers.

**Working Class Dogs, Inc.**
- Address: 828 North River Rd., McHenry, IL 60050
- Phone: (815) 653-3647
- Website: http://www.workingclassdogs.com
- Types of Animals Trained: Guide, Hearing, Mobility, Psychiatric, Other
- Services Provided: multiple disabilities, train handler, take donations, test and provide ID, children
- Comments: Provides services nationally. Also trains facility dogs - physical, occupational, recreational, emotional therapy facilities and social service agencies.

## ASSISTANCE DOGS INTERNATIONAL MEMBERS

The objective of Assistance Dogs International, Inc. is to establish and promote standards of excellence in all areas of Assistance Dog acquisition, training and partnership. The following organizations are fully accredited by ADI.

**Assistance Dog Institute**
- Address: 1215 Sebastopol Rd., Santa Rosa, CA 95407
- Phone: (707) 545-DOGS (3647)
- Fax: (707) 545-0800
- Website: http://assistancedog.org
- Dogs Trained: Service, Social
- Area Served: USA

**Assistance Dogs Australia**
- Address: P.O. Box 455, Engadine, NSW 2233
- Country: Australia
- Phone: (02)9548 3355
- Fax: (02)9548 1949
- Dogs Trained: Service, Therapy
- Other: Companion, Facility
- Area Served: Australia

**Assistance Dogs of America, Inc.**
- Address: 8806 State Route 64, Swanton, OH 43558
- Phone: (419) 825-3622
- Fax: (419) 825-3710
- Website: http://www.adai.org
- Dogs Trained: Service, Therapy
- Area Served: 250 mile radius of Northwest Ohio

**Assistance Dogs of the West**
- Address: P.O. Box 31027, Santa Fe, NM 87594
- Phone: (505) 986-9748
- Fax: (505) 986-9748
- Website: http://www.assistancedogsofthewest.org
- Dogs Trained: Service, Social, Therapy
- Other: Facility
- Area Served: Southwest Region of the U.S. and case by case for national

**Association of Australian Service Dogs (NQ), Inc.**
- Address: P.O. Box 2052, Mareeba North Queensland, 4872
- Country: Australia
- Phone: 61 0740935265
- Fax: 61 0740922359
- Website: http://www.asdogsnq.org
- Dogs Trained: Service, Seizure, Social, Therapy
- Other: Hypo Alert
- Area Served: Queensland, Australia

**Blue Ridge Assistance Dogs**
- Address: 8600 Smith Lane, Manassas, VA 20112
- Phone: (703) 369-5878
- Fax: (703) 369-5878
- Dogs Trained: Service, Seizure, Social, Therapy
- Area Served: VA, DC, MD, children in all states

**C.H.A.M.P Assistance Dogs, Inc.**
- Address: 4910 Parker Rd., Florissant, MO 63033
- Phone: (314) 653-9466
- Fax: (314) 653-1718
- Website: http://www.champdogs.org
- Dogs Trained: Service, Therapy
- Area Served: St. Louis and surrounding areas

**Canine Companions For Independence**
- Address: P.O. Box 446, Santa Rosa, CA 95402-0446
- Phone: (707) 577-1700 V; (707) 577-1756 TDD/TTY: (800) 572-2275
- Fax: (707) 577-1711
- Dogs Trained: Service, Hearing, Social
- Other: Facility
- Area Served: U.S.A. and Canada
- Comments: provides workshops for puppy raisers

**Canine Hearing Companions, Inc**
- Address: 247 E. Forest Grove Rd., Vineland, NJ 08360
- Phone: (856) 696-3668 V/TTY
- Fax: (856) 696-5405
- Dogs Trained: Hearing, Seizure, Therapy
- Other: Medical Alert
- Area Served: New Jersey, Pennsylvania, and Delaware

**Canine Partners**
- Address: Mill Lane, Heyshott, Midhurst, West Sussex GU29 0ED
- Country: England
- Phone: 011-44-8456 580480
- Fax: 011-44-8456 580 481
- Dogs Trained: Service, Seizure Response, Social
- Area Served: United Kingdom

**Canine Partners For Life**
- Address: P.O. Box 170, Cochranville, PA 19330-0170
- Phone: (610) 869-4902
- Fax: (610) 869-9785
- Website: http://www.k94life.org
- Dogs Trained: Service, Seizure, Social
- Area Served: 250 mile radius of facility/ will consider U.S.

**Canine Support Teams Inc.**
- Address: P.O. Box 956, Temecula, CA 95632-0950
- Phone: (209) 745-3701
- Fax: (209) 745-3007
- Website: http://www.caninesupportteams.org
- Dogs Trained: Service, Hearing, Mobility
- Other: Assisted Service, Facility
- Area Served: National and International provided individual is able to travel to Canine Support Teams.

**Canine Working Companions, Inc**
- Address: P.O. Box 2128, Syracuse, NY 13220
- Phone: (315) 656-3301
- Fax: (315) 656-3301
- Website: http://www.canineworkingcompanions.org
- Dogs Trained: Service, Hearing, Therapy
- Area Served: New York state excluding Buffalo and New York City

**Dogs For The Deaf, Inc.**

- Address: 10175 Wheeler Rd.,
  Central Point, OR 97502
- Phone: (541) 826-9220 (V/TDD)
- Fax: (541) 826-6696
- Website: http://www.dogsforthedeaf.org
- Dogs Trained: Hearing, Therapy
- Area Served: U.S. and Canada

**Dogs For The Disabled**

- Address: The Frances Hay Centre,
  Blacklocks Hill; Banbury,
  Oxfordshire OX17 2BS
- Country: United Kingdom
- Phone: 08700 776600
- Fax: 08700 776601
- Website: http://www.dogsforthedisabled.org
- Dogs Trained: Service
- Other: Skilled Companion
- Area Served: England and Wales

**East Coast Assistance Dogs**

- Address: 149 Newfield Rd.,
  Torrington, CT 06790
- Phone: (860) 489-6550
- Fax: (860) 489-3791
- Dogs Trained: Service, Social
- Area Served: Connecticut, New York, Massachusetts, Florida, Ohio, New Jersey, and Rhode Island

**Fidos For Freedom, Inc.**

- Address: P.O. Box 5508,
  Laurel, MD 20726
- Phone: (410) 880-4178 (V);
  TTY (301) 570-7570; (301) 490-4005 (V)
- Fax: (301) 490-9061
- Dogs Trained: Service, Hearing, Therapy
- Area Served: 75 mile radius of Laurel, MD

**Florida Dog Guides For The Deaf, Inc.**

- Address: P. O. Box 20662,
  Bradenton, FL 34204
- Phone: (941) 748-8245 (TDD);

(800) 520-4589
- Fax: (941) 747-0969
- Dogs Trained: Service, Hearing
- Area Served: Florida

**Freedom Service Dogs, Inc.**

- Address: P.O. Box 150217,
  Lakewood, CO 80215-0217
- Phone: (303) 922-6231
- Fax: (303) 922-6234
- Dogs Trained: Service
- Area Served: Colorado

**Great Plains Assistance Dogs Foundation**

- Address: P.O. Box 513,
  Jud, ND 58454-0513
- Phone: (877) 737-8364
- Fax: (701) 685-2290
- Website: http://greatplainsdogs.com
- Dogs Trained: Service, Seizure, Social, Therapy
- Other: Multi-task
- Area Served: U.S.

**Guide Dogs for the Blind, Inc.**

- Address: P.O. Box 151200,
  San Rafael, CA 94915-1200
- Phone: (415) 499-4000; (800) 295-4050
- Fax: (415) 499-4035
- Website: http://www.guidedogs.com
- Dogs Trained: Guide
- Areas Served: North America

**Guide Dog Foundation for the Blind, Inc.**

- Address: 371 East Jericho Turnpike,
  Smithtown, NY 11787
- Phone: (631) 930-9000; (800) 548-4337
- Fax: (631) 930-9009
- Dogs Trained: Guide
- Areas Served: North America

**Guide Dogs for the Blind Association**

- Address: Hillfields, Burghfield Commons,
  Reading; Berks, RG7 3YG

- Country: United Kingdom
- Phone: 00 44 1189 838 290
- Fax: 00 44 1189 838 290
- Website: http://www.gdba.org.uk
- Dogs Trained: Guide
- Area Served: All UK

**Happy Tails Service Dogs**
- Address: 1 West Sequoia Dr., Phoenix, AZ 85027
- Phone: (623) 580-0946
- Fax: (623) 581-3385
- Dogs Trained: Service
- Area Served: Arizona-Phoenix Area

**Hearing & Service Dogs of Minnesota**
- Address: 2537 25th Ave. South, Minneapolis, MN 55406
- Phone: (612) 729-5986 V: TDD (612) 729-5914
- Fax: (612) 729-5914
- Dogs Trained: Service, Hearing, Seizure
- Area Served: Minnesota

**Hearing Dogs for Deaf People**
- Address: The Grange, Wycombe Road; Sauderton Princes Risborough, Bucks, HP27 9NS
- Country: United Kingdom
- Phone: 011-44-844 348100
- Fax: 011-44-844 348101
- Dogs Trained: Hearing
- Area Served: United Kingdom / National

**Helping Paws of Minnesota**
- Address: 11 North 7th Ave., Hopkins, MN 55343
- Phone: (952) 988-9359
- Fax: (952) 988-9296
- Dogs Trained: Service
- Area Served: Minnesota and Northeast Wisconsin

**Japan Guide Dog Assn.**
- Address: Tsujido Eastcost 2-4-24,

Fujisawa City
- Country: Japan
- Phone: 00-81-466-35-7524
- Fax: 00-81-466-35-7524
- Dogs Trained: Guide
- Area Served: Japan

**Japan Hearing Dogs For Deaf People**
- Address: 3200 Miyada Kami-Ina, Nagano, 399-4301
- Country: Japan
- Phone: 81 265 85 4615
- Fax: 81 265 85 5290
- Dogs Trained: Hearing
- Area Served: Japan

**Kids and Canines**
- Address: 3215 Nundy Rd., Tampa, FL 33618
- Phone: (813) 558-5406
- Fax: (813) 558-5406
- Website: http://www.kidsandcanines.org
- Dogs Trained: Service, Therapy
- Area Served: Hillsborough County, Florida, and surrounding area

**KSDS, Inc.**
- Address: 124 West 7th St., Washington, KS 66968
- Phone: (785) 325-2256
- Fax: (785) 325-2258
- Website: http://www.ksds.org
- Dogs Trained: Service, Guide
- Area Served: U.S.

**Loving Paws Assistance Dogs**
- Address: P.O. Box 12005, Santa Rosa, CA 95406
- Phone: (707) 569-7092
- Fax: (707) 569-7270
- Website: http://www.lovingpaws.com
- Dogs Trained: Service, Social
- Area Served: U.S. and Canada

**National Service Dog Training Ctr., Inc.**
- Address: 28009 P.P.O.; Cambridge, Ontario, N3H 5N4
- Country: Canada
- Phone: (519) 623-4188
- Fax: (519) 623-9997
- Website: http://www.nsd.on.ca
- Dogs Trained: Service, Guide
- Other: Autism
- Area Served: International

**N. E. A. D. S.**
- Address: P.O. Box 213, West Boylston, MA 01583
- Phone: (978) 422-9064 V/TDD
- Fax: (978) 422-3255
- Dogs Trained: Service, Hearing, Social
- Other: Classroom Dogs
- Area Served: U.S.

**New Horizons Service Dogs**
- Address: 1590 Laurel Park Court, Orange City, FL 32763
- Phone: (386) 456-0408
- Fax: (386) 456-0409
- Website: http:// geocities.com/newhorizonsservicedogs/
- Dogs Trained: Service, Social
- Area Served: Florida

**New Life Assistance Dogs**
- Address: P.O. Box 10485, Lancaster, PA 17605-0485
- Phone: (717) 397-1841, (800) 995-9581
- Fax: (717) 293-1595
- Dogs Trained: Service
- Area Served: areas surrounding Lancaster, Pennsylvania

**Okada Specialty Guide Dogs**
- Address: 7509 E. Saviors Path, Floral City, FL 34436
- Phone: (540) 635-3937
- Fax: (352) 344-0210
- Website: okadadogs.com
- Dogs Trained: Hearing, Seizure, Therapy
- Other: Alzheimer's and Residential Therapy
- Area Served: U.S.-emphasis Florida

**Pacific Assistance Dog Society**
- Address: 9048 Stormont, Burnaby, BC V3N 4G6
- Country: Canada
- Phone: (604) 527-0556 (V/TDD)
- Fax: (604) 527-0558 (TDD/TTY)
- Website: http://www.padsdogs.org
- Dogs Trained: Service, Hearing, Therapy
- Area Served: Western Canada

**Paws With A Cause**
- Address: 4646 South Division, Wayland, MI 49348
- Phone: (616) 877-7297; 800-253-7297 TDD: (616) 877-7297
- Fax: (616) 877-0248
- Dogs Trained: Service, Hearing, Seizure, Social
- Area Served: U.S.

**Paws'itive Teams**
- Address: P.O. Box 27018, San Diego, CA 92198
- Phone: (858) 674-0845
- Fax: (858) 674-7461
- Dogs Trained: Service
- Area Served: San Diego County, California

**Prison Pet Partnership Program**
- Address: 9601 Bujacich Rd. NW, Gig Harbor, WA 98332
- Phone: (253) 858-4674
- Fax: (253) 858-4200
- Dogs Trained: Service, Seizure, Therapy
- Area Served: Washington, Oregon, Idaho

**Saint Francis of Assisi Service Dog Foundation**
- Address: P.O. Box 19538, Roanoke, VA 24019
- Phone: (540) 342-3647
- Fax: (540) 324-0906
- Dogs Trained: Service, Hearing, Social
- Area Served: Virginia

**Samsung Assistance Dog Services**
- Address: 310 Jeondae- Ri, Pokog-Myun, Yongin-Si, Kyonggi-Do
- Country: Korea
- Phone: 82 31 320 9222
- Fax: 82 31 320 8934
- Dogs Trained: Service, Hearing, Social
- Area Served: South Korea

**San Francisco SPCA Hearing Dog Program**
- Address: 2500 16th St., San Francisco, CA 94103
- Phone: (415) 554-3000
- Fax: (415) 552-7041
- Dogs Trained: Hearing
- Area Served: California and Nevada

**Sterling Service Dogs**
- Address: 5440 Brookdale, Bloomfield Hills, MI 48304
- Phone: (586) 977-9716
- Fax: (586) 977-0079
- Dogs Trained: Service, Social
- Area Served: U.S.A.

**Summit Assistance Dogs**
- Address: 7575 Chestnut Lane, Anacortes, WA 98221
- Phone: (360) 293-5609
- Fax: (360)293-5609
- Website: http://www.summitdogs.org
- Dogs Trained: Service, Hearing, Therapy
- Area Served: primarily Washington State

**Support Dogs**
- Address: 21 Jessops Riverside, Brightside Lane; Sheffield, S9 2RX
- Country: England
- Phone: 0870 609 3476
- Fax: 0114 2617 555
- Website: http://www.support-dogs.org.uk
- Dogs Trained: Service, Seizure
- Area Served: United Kingdom

**Susquehanna Service Dogs**
- Address: 3700 Vartan Way, Harrisburg, PA 17112
- Phone: (717) 599-5920
- Fax: (717) 541-5233
- Website: http://keystonehumanservices.org/ssd/ssd.php
- Dogs Trained: Service, Hearing, Social
- Area Served: Pennsylvania and surrounding area

**Texas Hearing and Service Dogs**
- Address: 4803 Rutherglen Dr., Austin, TX 78749-3744
- Phone: (512) 891-9090; (877) TEX-DOGS
- Fax: (512) 891-9090
- Website: http://www.servicedogs.org
- Dogs Trained: Service, Hearing
- Area Served: Texas

**Therapetics Service Dogs of Oklahoma**
- Address: 7717 E 21st Street, Suite B, Tulsa OK 74129
- Phone: (918) 270-4226; (866) 362-3647
- Fax: (918) 270-2285
- Website: http://www.therapetics.org
- Dogs Trained: Service, Social
- Area Served: Oklahoma

**Top Dog**
- Address: 5049 E. Broadway #102, Tucson, AZ 85711
- Phone: (520) 323-6677; (888) 257-6790
- Fax: (520) 323-3512

- Website: http://www.topdogusa.org
- Dogs Trained: Service
- Area Served: Tucson, AZ

**Verein Partner-Hunde Osterreich**
- Address: Weltworth 1, 5110 Oberndorf; Austria, Europe
- Country: Austria
- Phone: 43 6272 7706
- Fax: 43 6272 5299
- Website: http://www.partner-hunde.org
- Dogs Trained: Service, Hearing, Social, Therapy
- Area Served: Austria and Germany

*Melissa, Marcie and Morgan. Photo by Doug Reeves.*

# ABOUT THE AUTHORS

## MARCIE DAVIS

Marcie Davis is a writer, public speaker, advocate, and activist. She is the Chief Executive Officer of Davis Innovations, a public health and human service consulting firm that specializes in program development, policy, research, and advocacy. Marcie has been a paraplegic for over 35 years and has been partnered with a service dog for over thirteen years. She holds a Masters Degree in Library Science from the University of Southern Mississippi and has received numerous awards and accolades for her tireless advocacy on behalf of individuals who can not advocate for themselves. Marcie lives with her husband, Franz, and service dog, Morgan, in Santa Fe, New Mexico.

## MELISSA BUNNELL

Melissa Bunnell holds a Masters Degree in Social Work from The Ohio State University and has specialized in family and crisis counseling. As an animal lover she became interested in the subject of service dogs through her colleague and friend Marcie Davis, a service dog recipient. For over five years she has researched service dog resources and interviewed service dog partners, veterinarians and other professionals in the dog world and in 2003 co-founded Working Like Dogs, LLC, an organization dedicated to working dogs around the world. She lives with her husband and daughter in Santa Fe, New Mexico.

# INDEX*